MACBETH

WILLIAM SHAKESPEARE

PEACOCK BOOKS

Published by
PEACOCK BOOKS
7/22, Ansari Road, Darya Ganj, New Delhi-110002
Phones : +91-11-40775252, 40775214, 23273880, 23275880
Fax : +91-11-23285873
Web : www.atlanticbooks.com
E-mail : orders@atlanticbooks.com

Peacock Books is an imprint of
Atlantic Publishers and Distributors (P) Ltd

First published 1623

Printed & bound in India by Atlantic Print Services

CONTENTS

SHAKESPEARE'S PLAYS WITH THEIR PROBABLE APPROXIMATE DATES

There is absence of total agreement on the dates of Shakespearean plays. Some scholars give an earlier date than the one suggested here for Shakespeare's first play. Doubt also remains concerning the actual order of composition in particular years. Having stated that, the editor gives hereunder the approximate dates as largely accepted by Shakespeare scholars in general.

1590-91

Henry VI Part II
Henry VI Part III

1591-92

Henry VI
Part I

1592-93

Richard III
Comedy of Errors

1593-94

Titus Andronicus
Taming of the Shrew

1594-95

Two Gentlemen of
Verona
Love's Labour's Lost
Romeo and Juliet

1595-96

Richard II
Midsummer Night's
Dream

1596-97

King John
Merchant of Venice

1597-98

Henry IV Part I

Henry IV Part II

1598-99

Much Ado About Nothing

Henry V

1599-1600

Julius Caesar

As You Like It

Twelfth Night

1600-1601

Hamlet

Merry Wives of Windsor

1601-02

Troilus and Cressida

1602-03

All's Well That Ends Well

1604-05

Measure for Measure

Othello

1605-06

King Lear

Macbeth

1606-07

Antony and Cleopatra

1607-08

Coriolanus

Timon of Athens

1608-09

Pericles

1609-10

Cymbeline

1610-11

Winter's Tale

1611-12

The Tempest

1612-13

Henry VIII

Two Noble Kinsmen

WILLIAM SHAKESPEARE
BIOGRAPHICAL SKETCH

1. A Symbol of Culture

Introducing Shakespeare to the general reader, G.B. Harrison begins his book with the following statement :

> No household in the English-speaking world is properly furnished unless it contains copies of the *Holy Bible* and of *The Works of William Shakespeare*. It is not always thought necessary that these books should be read in maturer years, but they must be present as symbols of Religion and Culture.

Not only in the English speaking world, but everywhere, acquaintance with Shakespeare's plays is regarded as a mark of culture; and there is hardly any language-community in the civilized world, which does not possess Shakespeare in translation.

2. Life

Anyone looking for reliable historical information about Shakespeare is bound to meet with disappointment. We get very little help from his contemporaries in the form of recorded reference allusion, or memoirs, Shakespeare himself is completely silent about himself, and as regards his works, he has consumed himself into them so perfectly that it is very risky to draw any clear inferences from his works—except, perhaps, the sonnets, some of which, departing from the convention, appear to be expressing personal experience. We do, however, get some definite information from the parish register, legal documents and town records.

At first sight, it may appear astonishing that such a great writer as Shakespeare should have received no notice from his contemporaries and that no attempt should have been made to preserve every bit of the records associated with his life. But a second look at the state of affairs and attitude to biography prevailing in that period will mollify our uneasiness. The Elizabethans, generally, were indifferent to biographical and autobiographical notes and memoirs; even the biography of the most important personage, Queen Elizabeth herself, is full of gaps and guesses. It should, in fact, be gratifying that we possess more of authentic information about Shakespeare than about any of his contemporary writers excepting Ben Jonson. Moreover, Shakespeare, until very late in his life, was a very ordinary individual belonging to the socially unwelcome profession of actor; and the playwrights, too, were not much distinguished in the society. The critical response to his work was not unmixed high praise until the end of the eighteenth century. It was only in the beginning of the nineteenth century that Shakespeare became established as a great writer who must be spoken of with a feeling of reverence. But during the intervening centuries, he had been steadily moving towards the highest position, and as this process advanced, his admirers became over enthusiastic to complete his biography. The result was an infusion of a great deal of guesswork aggrandisement and romanticising. In such a situation, the best policy will be to keep close to the attested facts and reasonable inferences, except in cases where a highly dubious anecdote may, nevertheless, indicate some important turn in the dramatist's life.

William Shakespeare—the surname is found spelled in various other ways, which was not unusual in those days—was the son of John Shakespeare of Stratford-on-Avon. In 1556 John Shakespeare bought a house in Henley Street. In 1552, he, along with two neighbours, had been fined for keeping an unauthorized dunghill on Henley Street, which means he had been dwelling there for some years before he bought the house. In 1557 he married Mary Arden, the daughter of Robert Arden, a land-owning farmer who lived in Wilmcote, a small village two miles from Stratford. Mary brought with her an inheritance of sixty acres of land.

John Shakespeare was a glove-maker and dealer in wool, he may have at one time or another, pursued some other trades as well. He was a prosperous citizen of Stratford and one of its notables.

In the year of William Shakespeare's birth, however, his father was a prosperous businessman who was also a man of substance and of social standing. William, the third and surviving child of John and Mary Shakespeare was baptized on 26 April 1564. Allowing the usual period of three days between birth and baptism, it is generally assumed that William Shakespeare was born on 23 April 1564, which is also the day of the feast of St. George, the patron saint of England—and this is also the day on which Shakespeare breathed his last. The Shakespeares had five more children. It requires no documentary evidence to say that Shakespeare during his childhood observed and absorbed the life of town and village surging all around him and, possessing a rare talent, he stored in his mind sights, sounds, scenes and characters, which, combined with his experience of London, would prove a rich material at the forge of his creativity, when he came to write poems and plays.

There is no valid reason to doubt that William was enrolled in the local grammar school when he was six or seven years old. His father was still a prominent citizen and an important member of the borough council. But the school records for the period are not available. Nicholas Rowe, who brought out the first edited collection of Shakespeare's plays, wrote in his introduction that the boy studied in a free school where "it is probable, he acquired what Latin he was master of, but the narrowness of his circumstances, and the want of his assistance at home, forced his father to withdraw him from thence, and unhappily prevented his further proficiency in that language". John Aubrey a seventeenth-century antiquarian and biographer, in his *Brief Lives* published posthumously in 1813, informs us that Shakespeare had been a school master in a country school.

There is, however, no confusion regarding his early marriage to Anne Hathaway, who was about eight years his senior. One thing that can be safely inferred is that Shakespeare was an impetuous and highly romantic young man and this conclusion gets ample support in the essential nature of all his writings—they are romantic through and through. On 26th May 1583, their first issue Susanna was baptized in Stratford and two years later, the twins, Hamnet and Judith were born and christened on 2 February 1585. Of these children of Shakespeare, Hamnet died in 1596, Susanna married a physician named John Hall and inherited a major portion of her father's assets, Judith married Thomas Quiney.

The period from 1585 to 1592 in Shakespeare's life is known as the "dark years" or "lost years" from the biographer's point of view. For this period we have no authentic information about the family apart from a single reference to John Shakespeare in 1588 in connection with a legal dispute over a sum of money. There is, however, no dearth of legend and hearsay. According to Nicholas Rowe, Shakespeare incurred the wrath of the local landlord, Sir Thomas Lucy for stealing deer in his park and was, as a result, obliged to flee to London.

Though there are many conjectures, yet what sounds most credible is that Shakespeare attached himself to one of the touring theatrical companies that visited the countryside during the period under consideration. Three such companies, the Earl of Worcester's Men, the Earl of Oxford's Men and the Earl of Essex's Men, were giving performances at Stratford in 1581 and in 1585 the town people were entertained by an unidentified company. In 1587, the year in which Shakespeare most probably left his home town, the Earl of Essex's Men and the Earl of Leicester's Men were in Stratford; he might have accompanied one of these groups to London.

In the midst of financial and other problems besetting the family, joining a company of actors must have appealed to Shakespeare as a good expedient because it would bring some wages as well as give him an access to the literary world of London.

By 1592 Shakespeare's struggle had begun to bear fruit; in that year he was worthy enough to arouse the jealousy of another playwright, Robert Greene, one of the University Wits. In a letter addressed to his fellow writers and appended to a pamphlet called *Greene's Groatsworth of Wit Bought with a Million of Repentance* he made a scurrilous attack on Shakespeare for presuming to be not only an actor but the best playwright.

It is clear that by 1592 Shakespeare had established himself in London as an actor and dramatist : he had completed at least the three plays comprising the *Henry VI* trilogy; he had also probably been improving and retouching existing plays and there might have been some talk of his writing then in progress. Some scholars have argued that he had also completed or was about to complete *The Two Gentlemen of Verona, The Comedy of Errors, The Taming of the Shrew, Richard III, Titus Andronicus* and *Love's Labour's Lost*.

The next year, 1593, saw the publication of a long narrative poem, *Venus and Adonis*, with a signed dedication to Henry Wriothesley, the third Earl of Southampton : Your Honour's in all duty, William Shakespeare". In the following year came out another poem, *The Rape of Lucrece*, also dedicated to the same lord. This was the period during which the London theatres remained closed on account of the plague; that Shakespeare did not waste his time, but was busy writing poetry shows with what earnestness he pursued his aim of achieving literary renown. He had also started writing his sonnets during this period and some scholars have suggested that the group of sonnets addressed to a young man had the Earl of Southampton for their inspirator.

The theatres reopened in 1594 and staging of plays including some by Shakespeare began. We find that he is already an important member of Lord Chamberlain's company as disclosed by the following entry in the Chamber Accounts :

> To William Kemp, William Shakespeare, and Richard Burbage, servants to the Lord Chamberlain, upon the Council's warrant dated at Whitehall 15 March 1594 (-5) for two several comedies or interludes showed by them before her Majesty in Christmas time last past, *viz.* upon St. Stephen's day and Innocent's day, £ 13 6s, 8d, and by way of her Majesty's reward £ 6 13s, 4d.

From recorded references, allusions and lists of actors prefixed to printed plays, we gather that Shakespeare continued to act on the stage at least up to 1603 and if we rely on his fellow-actors, John Heminge and Henry Condell, who edited the First Folio edition of his plays in 1623, up to 1611. He is said to have played kingly roles including the Ghost in *Hamlet* but he also acted the part of old servant Adam in *As You Like It*. According to Aubrey, he "did act exceedingly well".

All the while Shakespeare was making steady progress in writing plays and in earning money and fame. During 1595-96, five of his new plays were produced : *Richard II, Romeo and Juliet, King John, A Midsummer Night's Dream,* and *The Merchant of Venice*. During the latter year there was a tragedy in the family : his only son Hamnet died in August 1596. In the same year, there was some more trouble for Shakespeare : according to a reference discovered by Leslie Hotson in 1931, one William Wayt claimed sureties of the peace against William Shakespeare and some other persons including Francis Langley then owner of the Swan Theatre. But his financial position was quite sound. He was living in a large house in Bishopsgate as the tax-rolls indicate, perhaps his family also stayed with him for brief periods. There is evidence of his purchase of property in London and in his hometown.

While living in London, Shakespeare appears to have maintained good links with his native place and its people. His narrative poems had been printed by Richard Field who had migrated from Stratford. In 1597 Shakespeare bought the largest house in Stratford, called New Place, from William Underhill for a sum of £ 60. On October 25, 1598, Richard Quiney a Stratford man who was visiting London wrote a letter to Shakespeare requesting a loan of £ 30. In 1599 the famous actor, Richard Burbage and his brother Cuthbert set up a new playhouse on the Bankside, called the Globe. Since they could not finance the project on their own, they invited some other members of their company, Lord Chamberlain's Men, to become shareholders. Shakespeare thus became a part-owner of the Globe, entitled to ten per cent of the profits. He enjoyed the unique privilege of being a dramatist, actor and businessman.

During the period 1597-99 six more plays comprising comedies and plays on English history were produced : *Merry Wives of Windsor, Much Ado About Nothing, As You Like It, Henry IV-Part One, Henry IV-Part Two,* and *Henry V*, probably *Julius Caesar* also had its first staging in 1599.

The new century opened with a personal tragedy to Shakespeare : his father died in 1601. It also brought him to the threshold of his tragic vision—the truest and profoundest ever presented to theatre audiences and to the readers of the world. Before the death of Queen Elizabeth in 1603, the greatest, tragedy of personal dilemma *Hamlet* had its first performance. His finest comedy, *Twelfth Night* and the 'problem play' *Troilus and Cressida* were also produced before 1603. With the accession of King James to the English throne, Lord Chamberlain's Men, evidently regarded as the best company of actors, was taken under royal patronage and was renamed King's Men. The letters patent issued on 19 May 1603 mention William Shakespeare along with some other members of the company including Heminge and Condell, the future editors of the first edition of his Collected Plays. The actors of the company became eligible to special privileges; records indicate that they were often called upon to present plays before the Court and to participate in royal pageants and processions—several Shakespeare plays were performed at the Court. In March 1604, when King James made a 'royal proceeding' through the city of London, Shakespeare—as well as each of his fellow players—was given four yards of red cloth for his livery.

On the plane of worldly affairs too, Shakespeare was faring very well. In may 1602 he purchased one hundred and seven acres of arable land to the parish of old Stratford and in September he acquired a cottage in Chapel Lane, Stratford-on-Avon. A fellow actor, Augustine Phillipps, when he made his will in May 1605, mentioned Shakespeare first among the recipients of his bequests of gold pieces : "I give and bequeath to my fellow, William Shakespeare, a thirty-shilling piece in gold." Two years later in 1607 his favourite daughter Susanna, married the physician John Hall and in February 1608 their daughter Elizabeth was born. It is almost certain that Edmond Shakespeare whose burial is recorded in the registers of the Church of St. Saviours in Southwark was the poet's brother. Shakespeare's mother died in 1608.

In Shakespeare's literary output, the period 1604-1608 is the period of great tragedies : *Othello, Macbeth, King Lear, Antony and Cleopatra* and *Cariolanus.* The other plays first produced during this period are : *Measure for Measure, All is Well That Ends Well* and *Timon of Athens.* Some scholars, however, believe that *All's Well That Ends Well* is an early play, perhaps *Love's Labour's Won,* mentioned by Francis Meres in his *Palladis Tamia* (1598).

In 1608 the King's Men took over the Blackfriars, an indoor theatre where Henry Evans's children's company had been staging plays since 1600. Shakespeare thus began writing plays for both Blackfriars and the Globe. He appears to have adjusted himself to the conditions and upper-class audiences at the Blackfriars. Otherwise, too, Shakespeare about this time had emerged from the Inferno of human and supernatural evil. He had explored the genesis, nature, working and consequences of evil and expressed them in the best of utterance. Now in the last phase of his career, he turned to superior kinds of solutions.

Evil keeps raising its head, but it is confronted by higher human nature and is overthrown without waste or destruction. This is the tenor of his last plays : *Pericles, Cymbeline, The Winter's Tale, The Tempest.*

William Shakespeare had made his life a grand success : Whatever wrongs, malice, envy or injury he had suffered were behind him; he had become rich and respected; thousands of human hearts had been moved to laughter and tears by the magic of his lines; he had learnt the last lesson in human wisdom.

Around 1611 Shakespeare contentedly retired to Stratford. His remaining two younger brothers, Gilbert and Richard died in 1612 and 1613 respectively. John Combe, one of his closest friends also died in 1613 leaving him a bequest of £ 5. On March 10, 1613, he bought the Blackfriar's Gate House.

Shakespeare did not break his relations completely with his company; he also kept visiting London from time to time. The last two plays which he wrote in collaboration with John Fletcher are *Henry VII* and *The Two Noble Kinsmen*, but his heart wasn't there; they suffer in execution and in imaginative power. Shakespeare's health began to deteriorate after 1613. According to one report some time in 1616 Drayton and Ben Jonson came down to visit him and they had a merry meeting. His will was drawn up in January 1616. Since his younger daughter Judith got married to Thomas Quiney on February 10, the will was revised and executed by him on March 25.

In his will, Shakespeare bequeathed nearly all his property to his elder daughter Susanna Hall and her husband; Judith his younger daughter received very little in comparison. Perhaps Shakespeare was not happy with Judith's marriage to Thomas

Quiney about whom there was some scandal, or, he feared any fixed assets made over to her would not remain secure, but he made provision for yearly payment of some money to her. This apparent lack of balance on the part of Shakespeare is bound to remind us of his own creation *King Lear*.

Another matter which causes surprise is the bequest to his wife. She is not mentioned by name and Shakespeare appears to have added one sentence about her as an after thought : "I give unto my wife my second best bed with the furniture". Those who defend Shakespeare on this issue argue that the best bed in the house would be reserved for guests, that he gave her the second best bed because it carried past associations since this must have been the bed the couple used to sleep in. It is also true that Anne's dower rights already stood protected bylaw; she must have continued to live in New Place until her death in 1623. And yet, when all this has been said, one cannot help feeling that this slighting gesture on the part of Shakespeare indicates that something had gone sour in their relations.

He left something to each of his relations: niece Elizabeth Hall, sister Joan and her three sons; he did not forget his friends and the poor of Stratford, to whom he bequeathed ten pounds. It is to be noted that he gave 26s. 8d. each to his former fellow actors, John Heminge, Richard Burbage and Henry Condell for buying mourning rings.

Shakespeare died on 23 April, 1616, but Death could not be proud of this, for in black ink his name still shines bright. A monument representing the poet in the act of writing with a quill was installed some time between his death and the year 1623. This is the famous bust with which the whole world has become familiar. The other authentic likeness is Martin Droeshout's engraving on the title page of the First Folio Collection of

Shakespeare's Plays, which is equally familiar to readers. The epitaph inscribed under the bust praises Shakespeare as a writer.

With whome
Quick nature died; whose name doth deck
this tombe
Far more than most, sith all that He hath writt
Leaves living art, but page, to serve his witt.

MACBETH

A CRITICAL INTRODUCTION

(i) INTRODUCING SHAKESPEARE, THE INDIVIDUAL AND THE PLAYWRIGHT AND THE AGE HE LIVED IN

Shakespeare is undoubtedly one of the greatest writers in the whole range of world literature. It would be interesting as well as instructive to place him in his personal, social and cultural context. Only then can one understand his plays fully and appreciate his achievement properly. William Shakespeare, the third child and the eldest son of John Shakespeare and Mary Arden, was born in April 1564. His father was one of the richest persons of Stratford upon Avon and he had held in turn the chief offices in the town. However, we hardly have details about William Shakespeare's early life and interests. One school of Shakespeare criticism holds that he fled from Stratford because he was in trouble for deer stealing and had fallen foul of Sir Thomas Lucy, the local magnate. However, there are other scholars who believe that Shakespeare had been a school-master for some time. We do have information to the effect that in his nineteenth year, Shakespeare married Ann Hathaway and his first child, Susanna was baptized in May 1583 and twins, Hamnet and Judith were baptized in February 1585.

The first reference to his budding literary career that the critics discovered was made in a letter that the dying Robert

Greene wrote in the autumn of 1592. It refers to Shakespeare's coming to sudden prominence. Mention may be made of Shakespeare's coming into contact with Edward Alleyne around this time. Alleyne was a great actor of the period and he had successfully played the roles of Tamburlaine, the Jew of Malta and Dr. Faustus—all the creations of Christopher Marlowe, Shakespeare predecessor in the field of English drama. Alleyne had also played the role of Hieronimo, the hero of Kyd's *Spanish Tragedy*, the most famous of all Elizabethan plays. This contact with the great tragedian must have influenced the young writer in Shakespeare. By this time he is believed to have written the major part of *Henry VI*.

Now we have regular record of his work. *Venus and Adonis* in April 1593 and *The Rape of Lucree* in May 1594—both dedicated to the young Earl of Southampton—established his literary credentials on very firm footing. When the theatres opened in 1594 after the Great Plague of 1593, Shakespeare became a sharer in Lord Chamberlaine's Company. Shakespeare's plays followed one after the other in seeming torrent and Marlowe and Kyd having died in early 1594, Shakespeare was the undisputed king of letters now. The list of his plays around this time, given separately, shows his coming to his own.

In 1597, Shakespeare's plays were being staged at Curtain until the erection of Globe Theatre on the South bank of the Thames. A very significant change took place in 1608 when plays came to be staged at an indoor private theatre in the fashionable quarters of the Blackfriars. Here plays were performed indoors; the prices charged were higher and the audience consequently was more select. It was here that Shakespeare tried his hand at the new form of tragi-comedy—a play with tragic incidents but a happy ending—which Beaumont and Fletcher had popularized. *Pericles*, *Cymbeline*, *The Winter's Tale* and *The Tempest* could have been possible at Blackfriars.

Meanwhile Shakespeare had bought New Place, a large house in the centre of Stratford and through his father purchased a coat-of-arms from the Heralds, which was the official recognition that he and his family were gentlefolk. Around this time a young writer named Francis Meres in his book *Palladis Tamia* paid Shakespeare a remarkable tribute, mentioning the names of twelve of his plays. After the death of Queen Elizabeth I on March 24, 1603, King James came to the throne and he actively patronized the theatre company, so that henceforward they were known as the King's Men. Shakespeare's sombre comedies, *All's Well That Ends Well, Measure for Measure;* followed by *Othello*, *Macbeth* and *King Lear* and later his return to the Roman themes in *Antony and Cleopatra* and *Coriolanus* owes a lot to the court atmosphere and patronage.

The coming of new playwrights like Ben Jonson on the literary scene in the early years of the seventeenth century, the coming to reckoning of other promising playwrights like Chapman, Dekker, Marston and Beaumont and Fletcher and perhaps the most significant factor of them all, the death of Shakespeare's son Hamnet in 1596 slowed down the writer in Shakespeare. His two daughters had also left him after getting married. Shakespeare eventually died on April 23, 1616 at Stratford upon Avon at the age of 52. His wife survived him.

It is also interesting to know something about the publication of Shakespeare's plays after his death. Fourteen of his plays had already been published in Quarto booklets when Shakespeare died. In 1623, Shakespeare's surviving fellow actors published a collected edition of thirty-six plays in one Folio Volume with memorial verses by Ben Jonson and others.

An Epistle to the Reader was also included wherein it was contended that Shakespeare's "hand and mind went together, and what he thought, he uttered with that easiness that we have scarce received from him a blot in his papers." The plays as printed in the Quartos or the Folio differ considerably from the usual modern text. There is hardly division of the text into scenes or even acts. Place-headings are also not provided at the beginning of each scene. The printing also is not meticulous and spellings are often erratic. It was much later that considerable scholarship went into each text to give it the shape that one finds at present, even though at quite a few places, editors differ on particular lines, words, scenes or even speeches attributed to the character concerned.

(ii) SHAKESPEARE'S CONCEPTION OF TRAGEDY

A Shakespearean tragedy, critics say, is a five storey mansion marked by exposition, the rising action, the crisis, the falling action and the catastrophe. Its hero rises from scene to scene on the currents of passion and imagination; having at last, reached the heights of tragedy, he disappears through death but only after highlighting the inherent greatness of man.

Shakespeare has written a large number of tragedies of which the four, *Hamlet, Macbeth, Othello* and *King Lear* are considered to be standard works for purposes of analysing his conception of tragedy. These, tragedies have, no doubt, different designs, but there is a family likeness in their heroes who have common traits and humours that constitute their characters.

The Shakespearean tragic protagonist is usually a great, high born personage. He towers above the rest in character and in action, issuing from that character. The action which proceeds mainly from character, brings about many unforeseen situations as a result of which many persons die. The tragedy therefore is the destruction of so much potential goodness in the destruction of evil.

Some critics believe that character is destiny in a Shakespearean tragedy. That is, the character of the hero determines his fate and destiny. This view places a Shakespearean tragedy in contrast with the conception of the Greek tragedy. In the latter, the hero is merely an agent of Fate, and not the master of his destiny. In a Greek tragedy, there are the gods who punish the hero; in a Shakespearean tragedy the hero is punished by his self-willed actions. The former works through fate, the latter through free will. This idea should not exclude the sense of Fate or Destiny from a Shakespearean tragedy. There is fate but this does not control the actions of the heroes. Man is free, in the world of Shakespearean tragedy, to choose, but having chosen once he cannot retract or retrace. The sequence of events set in motion by human actions marches majestically to the tragic end and there is the sense of fate in the relentless, inevitable march of these events :

"Our thoughts are ours; but their
ends none of our own"

The sense of Fate is present in the form of ghosts and witches which inhabit the world of Shakespearean tragedy. These are the symbols of the supernatural which is very artistically presented as both within the protagonist and without him. Hamlet's view given below has to be seen in this context :

"There is a divinity that shapes
Our ends : rough hew them as we will."

The same view is presented thus in *King Lear* :

"As flies to wanton boys are we to the gods;
They kill us for their sport."

The final impression is unmistakable that Fate as well as Free Will, Freedom and Necessity are both present in a Shakespearean tragedy. The emotion of the audience is a blend of both these feelings of the natural and the supernatural, the human and the divine.

The tragic action in a Shakespearean tragedy proceeds from the free will of the hero. Even though the hero possesses great qualities of head and heart, of will and imagination, he has a fatal flaw in his make up. This flaw is, quite often, an error of judgement, a slight particularity of one's being. He is essentially good, noble, virtuous and has faith in a divine order. But his very being comes in the way of his confronting his circumstances squarely. His functioning thereby becomes to some extent predictable, given his situation. Given such and such traits of character, we know, he must do such and such a deed. This is why it is called a fatal flaw.

The Shakespearean tragedy also arises out of the conflict between good and evil. In its effort to destroy evil, the conflict involves a huge waste of good as well. The tragedy therefore is in the waste of the good and the innocent in the wake of death which also destroys the evil and the guilty. The mighty rush of tragic action whose source is the fatal flaw in the hero's character, grinds innocent and the guilty alike. It is on this account that a critic has pointed out an utter lack of 'poetic justice' in a Shakespearean tragedy. The death of Desdemona in *Othello* and that of Cordelia in *King Lear* is caused by the forces of destruction unleashed by the tragic action of the hero.

The final impression left by witnessing a Shakespearean tragedy is not of terror or tragic waste. It is replaced, relieved by a sense of exaltation and appreciation for the nobility of the man who fights while he falls, and who redeems human nature by his flights of imagination, will and emotion. It restores the sublimity of man and his greatness in adversity. Shakespeare through his poetry provides a sort of relief to the sense of tragic loss. When we rise from our seats, we carry memories of the hero and the associates who reassure us out of our shaken and shocked feelings into joyful acceptance of life which with all its tears is yet potentially rich in possibilities. We have the feeling that it is better to have loved and lost than never to have had the opportunity of loving.

(iii) INTRODUCTION

Macbeth is one of the principal tragedies of Shakespeare, usually clubbed together with *Hamlet*, *Othello* and *King Lear*. It has all the attributes of a typical Shakespearean tragedy—an exalted protagonist who is above average in qualities of head and heart, a significant want in his being which proves fatal in the circumstances in which he is placed, a mixed series of events in which he appears sinning as well as sinned against, the latter more than the former if one were to apportion the two and, last but not least, a denouement which does have some elements of poetic justice even as the protagonist evokes a sense of immense tragic loss. One could perhaps also add that even though Macbeth goes down and is bettered by forces more powerful than him, his going down, far from making the readers feel depressed, underscores how grand, how irrepressible, how magnificent a human being is. As a phenomenon of nature, man may be but a creature, subject to other more potent powers but the manner in which man conducts himself makes even his defeat a victory.

(iv) THE ROLE OF EVIL IN THE PLAY

Macbeth is a discovery of anatomy of evil. Of all Shakespeare's plays, it is the one most obsessively concerned with evil. In earlier works evil certainly was there but it was a shadow placed amid sunlight, beside the radiance of Desdemona, Cordelia, Beatrice or the suffering-far-good of Titus and Othello. Here the evil is larger, more fascinating, more effective than the dim representation of good. Macbeth falls, but does not do so primarily because of the processes or power of his enemies. His black tyranny produces the engines of its own destruction; the movement that carries Malcolm, Macduff and Seyward above him is generated by his own downward tendency primarily and only secondarily by their efforts. Good struggles forward in the world of Macbeth; but evil is all-pervasive. Even in flight, individuals cannot escape from the hold of evil. It is as much within them as it is without.

(v) THE WITCHES

The play begins with the witches, and the witches do stand for one kind of evil; but the mode of evil they can create is potential only and not actual, till the human agent takes it inside his mind and makes it his own by a motion of the will. It is well demonstrated by the contrast of Macbeth and Banquo. The essential difference appears in the response of the two to the greeting of the witches. Macbeth is startled by the witches' greeting hailing him as a king. Banquo draws attention to it in Act I; Scene (iii) lines 50-51. The witches seem but a concretization of the evil in abstract in Macbeth. Banquo recognizes the evil and sees it as something threatening, but outside himself (lines 122-25 in the same scene). The suggestion of the witches 'starts' Macbeth because it finds an answering image inside his own mind. Banquo may have contemplated murder by occasionally allowing the thought to pass through his mind but such 'cursed thoughts' were dismissed as 'instruments of darkness'. Macbeth's sensory reaction, on the other hand, points not to a direct and uncompromising rejection of evil, but to a paralysis of the moral powers.

(vi) THE ROLE OF MACBETH

Macbeth's 'gift' for bloodshed, his 'overvaulting' ambition are : 'floating' qualities. But these get set in a predictable direction after the encounter with the witches. The witches hold up a mirror in which Macbeth sees his powers fulfilled in a strange way. He is "possessed" by the image of himself that the witches show. The chance to play host to the king comes soon enough but Lady Macbeth has to 'will' Macbeth to go ahead; though the actual performance is Macbeth's, the impulse comes from the wife. Henceforth "to know my deed 'twere best not known myself", says Macbeth to himself. The deed is done but the rest of Macbeth's life would be an attempt to live with its implications.

Macbeth still thinks himself to be in quest of the social good, a good that only needs the deaths of Banquo and Fleance to make it click into place. Even the flight of Fleance does not seem to matter to him. Macbeth operates all through by incessant falsehood or prevarication. He does not trust the assassins he sends to murder Banquo, for he sends a third murderer in their midst. He does not trust even his accomplice, his wife whom he asks to wait for and applaud the deed in Act III; Scene (ii), lines 45-46. It is not irrelevant to remind oneself at this juncture that it is again the witches who have 'exploited' Macbeth's vulnerability to evil by suggesting to him indirectly the way to ensure the continued enjoyment of his ambition. But the pretended social order soon breaks down as the Ghost of Banquo enters and the show breaks into a rout of order

"Stand not upon the order of your going;
But go at once" (lines 118-19)

(vii) THE ROLE OF LADY MACBETH

Lady Macbeth is never the same person after the Banquet Scene. True, Macbeth, recovers his poise as the Ghost vanishes but his social ruin is complete. His break with Lady Macbeth is total and hereafter he would climb out of his abyss by planning new exploits. With appalling clarity he now accepts the witches for what they are—'the Worst' (lines 134-35).

Act IV, Scene (i) is a very significant witch-scene, different from other such scenes. Macbeth seeks out the witches himself and he seems more adept, the way he seeks out physical details. He knows that his success is being bought by damnation but he does not care. He seems concerned only with his 'security' and for him moral status becomes irrelevant. The witches advise him to

"Be bloody, bold and resolute; laugh to scorn
The power of man; for none of woman born
Shall harm Macbeth"

in Act IV; Scene (i), lines 178-80. Macbeth resolves to eliminate Macduff, "His wife, his babes, and all unfortunate souls/That trace him in his line" in lines 149-52.

A very effective contrast is presented between two repositories of 'supernatural powers' in the play. Macbeth journeys to the novel to seek assurance from the witches. Macduff travels to the English court to find hope, to seek a cure for the horror of the recent past. The 'testing' of Macduff is in contrast to Macbeth's attempt to question the powers that speak to him. When the witches vanish, Macbeth is so lonely that he damns all those, including himself who depend on them. The witches 'infect' where they ride but King Edward disinfects. King Edward has a gift of prophecy; the prophetic powers of the witches come from hell.

Throughout the last Act, Macbeth clings to the sense of 'security' given to him by the witches, that he would not die by 'one of woman born'. But the enemies he has to face are not men who can be dealt with by arms or by the strength of a fortess. Within the impregnable fortess, we see his wife fall before a foe she cannot overcome, her conscience. It is despair that has turned Macbeth to stone. Macbeth exclaims, "I have lived long enough.... Life's but a walking shadow... I 'gin to be weary of the sun."

Macbeth loses so much of himself towards the close of the play that, it is interesting to note that hardly is the name 'Macbeth' used in the last Act-and-a-half. He is 'the tyrant'. From Malcolm's viewpoint, we look at the same thing from a social point of view : a disease has to be plucked out of the body politic. The imagery of the play is also notable from this perspective. It is lurid and violent—'shapes of horror, dimly seen in the murky air or revealed by the glare of the cauldron'. Darkness, fire, thunder, the world of the actor, the world of a man wearing clothes too grand for him—these are continuously invoked to give us the sense of an inferno barely concealed beneath the surface.

(viii) MACBETH AS A MAN, NOT A FIEND

The final exchange between Macbeth and Macduff points at a more complex valuation. Macbeth's refusal to fight with Macduff because

"...my soul is too much charged
With blood of thine already"

in Act V; Scene (vi), lines 44-45, is unexpected but not totally implausible, for the idea of a 'good' Macbeth, buried somewhere beneath the activities of a will dedicated to evil, does remain valid in the play. In Act V; Scene (iii), lines 24-25, for example, Macbeth is given a poet-like awareness of things which he cannot hope to have because of his actions, *viz.*, "honour, love, obedience, troops of friends". Macbeth is presented in the play as a man, not a fiend. Mention may be made here of the brief '*anagnorisis*', the sudden recognition of what the "juggling fiends" have done. Macbeth dies as he had begun the play, fighting manfully. But without the flinching, without the moment of *anagnorisis*, the final heroic resistance would not be fully human. This ensures that we detest not so much what he is, as what he has become, the process of damnation.

(ix) MACBETH OVER THE AGES : INTERPRETATION BY PERFORMANCE

One of the more popular plays of Shakespeare, *Macbeth* has been truthfully depicting the taste of the different ages it has been enacted in. It has undergone significant changes which constitute, in one sense, different interpretations given to its diverse facets—theme, action and characters. Presumably the part of Macbeth was played originally by Richard Burbage, who created the title roles of all the great Shakespeare tragedies. The constuming stayed contemporary up to and beyond the time of Garrick, who played the hero in the scarlet coat of an eighteenth-century general. But a sea-change was affected in 1772 when Macklin turned to dresses befitting the primitive nature of the action. Right since then barbaric clothing has prevailed reaching perhaps its inevitable conclusion in the

Orson Welles film of 1948 which set the play in the constumes of the reign of Genghis Khan.

Another significant change incorporated was in late seventeenth century by Sir William Davenant who gave the play a 'regular' or neo-classical character. Some superfluous characters like the old Man, the bleeding Captain and the Porter were either dropped or replaced by the universal factotum and confidant, Seyton. More significantly Davenant introduced a completely new witch scene, after Act II; Scene (iv). Here Lady Macduff meets her fleeing husband and both hear the witches prophesying to them as they had to Macbeth and Banquo earlier. The invention underscores what Shakespeare had been content with merely suggesting. This addition, together with other spectacular incorporations were presumably seen by Pepys in 1667 when he made the oft-quoted reference to *Macbeth* as "a most excellent play in all respects". Even after Garrick had deleted most of Davenant's changes in 1744, the play in its bare original form was not restored. Garrick had his own additions, most notable of them being the speech he gave to the dying Macbeth.

Not merely was *Macbeth* studded with external spectacle, the natural or internal spectacle of the play was also, in the process, reduced. In the Jacobean theatre, the appearance of Banquo's ghost in the banqueting scene was a much awaited sequence. But the rationalizing mind in the eighteenth century was caught in the clash between externalization of the hero's internal conflict and the physical presence of a ghostly being who is not seen by others present. The Elizabethan practice of using a dramatic convention in rather a crude form for affording a peep into the protagonist's mind, did not go well, and in J.P. Kemble's production of the play in 1794, it was dispelled, even as the Hecat scenes were given new splendour. Kemble's

Macbeth was an attempt to read the psychological nuances of the action staged even though the protagonist was still seen in the classical mould—slow-moving, dignified, suffering. But Lady Macbeth was projected on a significantly more attractive, more courteous, more forceful and more terrifying key by Kemble's sister, Mrs. Siddons. She imparted to the character a rare elevation, grandness and simplicity. However, in some respects, the character became too overbearing and too scornful of her husband's weakness to provide a truthful image of Shakespeare's Lady—of the wavering and deeply divided nature of one who destroys her own finer self in order to satisfy her husband's ambitions.

The Romantic version of the intrinsic dilemma of human spirit—the Childe-Harold-like alternation of extremes—was put forth by Edward Kean. The movement from noble to ignoble Macbeth was a fairly continuous nineteenth century movement. In Irving's interpretation of the play, the protagonist is seen as unmanned by guilt. This Macbeth, as he becomes unscrupulous and reckless, also becomes abject. In the encounter with Banquo's ghost, in one mid nineteenth century production, Macbeth throws his cloak over his face ("Hence, horrible shadow") and sinks back into his chair. In another performance, not merely does the protagonist throw his cloak over his face but also falls down at the foot of the throne. Even modern Macbeths, in some respects, continue to be, anxious, dismayed, hysterical and lacking in the stature that would terrify us.

Attempts to modernize *Macbeth* and present him in contemporary setting have not been successful. However, the plot of the play is clearly strong enough and archetypal enough to survive transposition into quite remote media. A rendering of the play into Chicago gang terms in America proved it beyond doubt. In a Japanese adaptation the effort to externalise Macbeth's mind in terms of visual images rather than words added a significant dimension to the play. The forest becomes a central metaphor in the play—at once an impediment in the way of the protagonist's conquest of the castle as well as a symbol of the natural barbarity of his mind. These adaptations of the play across the big cultural and linguistic barrier offer an interesting interpretation of the play as well. They stress the point that, by conquering the kingdom, Macbeth becomes what Duncan himself was—the object (rather than the subject) of ambition and treachery.

THE TRAGEDY OF MACBETH

THE ACTORS' NAMES

DUNCAN, King of Scotland

MALCOLM DONALBAIN	his sons
MACBETH BANQUO	generals of the King's army
MACDUFF LENNOX ROSS MENTEITH ANGUS CAITHNESS	noblemen of Scotland

FLEANCE, son to Banquo
SIWARD, Earl of Northumberland, general of the English forces
Young SIWARD, his son
SEYTON, an officer attending on Macbeth
Boy, son to Macduff
An English Doctor
A Scottish Doctor
A Captain
A Soldier
A Porter
An Old Man
Three murderers
LADY MACBETH
LADY MACDUFF
Gentlewoman attending on Lady Macbeth
HECATE
Three Witches
Apparitions
Lords, Gentlemen, Officers, Soldiers, Attendants, and Messengers

I. 1

Thunder and lightning. Enter three Witches.

FIRST WITCH: When shall we three meet again?
In thunder, lightning, or in rain?
SECOND WITCH: When the hurly-burly's done,
When the battle's lost, and won.
THIRD WITCH: That will be ere the set of sun.
FIRST WITCH: Where the place?
SECOND WITCH: Upon the Heath.
THIRD WITCH: There to meet with Macbeth.
FIRST WITCH: I come, Graymalkin.
ALL: Paddock calls anon:
Fair is foul, and foul is fair,
Hover through the fog and filthy air.

Exeunt.

I. 2

Alarum within. Enter King Duncan, Malcolm, Donalbain, Lennox, with Attendants, meeting a bleeding Captain.

DUNCAN: What bloody man is that? He can report,
As seemeth by his plight, of the revolt
The newest state.
MALCOLM: This is the Sergeant,
Who like a good and hardy soldier fought
'Gainst my captivity: hail brave friend;

Say to the King, the knowledge of the broil,
As thou didst leave it.
CAPTAIN: Doubtful it stood,
As two spent swimmers, that do cling together,
And choke their art. The merciless Macdonwald
(Worthy to be a rebel, for to that
The multiplying villanies of Nature
Do swarm upon him) from the Western Isles
Of kerns and gallowglasses is suppli'd,
And Fortune on his damned quarry smiling,
Show'd like a rebel's whore: but all's too weak:
For brave Macbeth (well he deserves that name)
Disdaining Fortune, with his brandish'd steel,
Which smok'd with bloody execution,
(Like Valour's minion) carv'd out his passage,
Till he fac'd the slave:
Which ne'er shook hands, nor bade farewell to him,
Till he unseam'd him from the nave to th' chops,
And fix'd his head upon our battlements.
DUNCAN: O valiant cousin, worthy gentleman.
CAPTAIN: As whence the sun 'gins his reflection,
Shipwracking storms, and direful thunders break:
So from that spring, whence comfort seem'd to come,
Discomfort swells. Mark King of Scotland, mark,
No sooner Justice had, with Valour arm'd,
Compell'd these skipping kerns to trust their heels,
But the Norweyan Lord, surveying vantage,
With furbish'd arms, and new supplies of men,
Began a fresh assault.
DUNCAN: Dismay'd not this our Captains, Macbeth and Banquo?
CAPTAIN: Yes, as sparrows eagles; or the hare the lion:
If I say sooth, I must report they were

As cannons overcharg'd with double cracks,
So they doubly redoubled strokes upon the foe:
Except they meant to bathe in reeking wounds,
Or memorize another Golgotha,
I cannot tell: but I am faint,
My gashes cry for help.
DUNCAN: So well thy words become thee, as thy wounds,
They smack of honour both: go get him surgeons.

Enter Ross and Angus.

Who comes here?
MALCOLM: The worthy Thane of Ross.
LENNOX: What a haste looks through his eyes!
So should he look, that seems to speak things strange.
ROSS: God save the King.
DUNCAN: Whence cam'st thou, worthy Thane?
ROSS: From Fife, great King,
Where the Norweyan banners flout the sky,
And fan our people cold.
Norway himself, with terrible numbers,
Assisted by that most disloyal traitor,
The Thane of Cawdor, began a dismal conflict,
Till that Bellona's bridegroom, lapp'd in proof,
Confronted him with self-comparisons,
Point against point, rebellious arm 'gainst arm,
Curbing his lavish spirit: and to conclude,
The victory fell on us.
DUNCAN: Great happiness.
ROSS : That now Sweno, the Norways' King,
Craves composition:
Nor would we deign him burial of his men,
Till he disbursed, at Saint Colme's Inch,
Ten thousand dollars, to our general use.
DUNCAN: No more that Thane of Cawdor shall deceive

Our bosom interest: go pronounce his present death,
And with his former title greet Macbeth.
ROSS: I'll see it done.
DUNCAN : What he hath lost, noble Macbeth hath won.
Exeunt.

I. 3

Thunder. Enter the three Witches.

FIRST WITCH: Where hast thou been, sister?
SECOND WITCH: Killing swine.
THIRD WITCH: Sister, where thou?
FIRST WITCH: A sailor's wife had chestnuts in her lap,
And mounch'd, and mounch'd, and mounch'd:
Give me, quoth I.
Aroint thee, witch, the rump-fed ronyon cries.
Her husband's to Aleppo gone, Master o' th' *Tiger*:
But in a sieve I'll thither sail,
And like a rat without a tail,
I'll do, I'll do, and I'll do.
SECOND WITCH: I'll give thee a wind.
FIRST WITCH: Th' art kind.
THIRD WITCH: And I another.
FIRST WITCH: I myself have all the other,
And the very ports they blow,
All the quarters that they know,
I' th' shipman's card.
I 'll drain him dry as hay:
Sleep shall neither night nor day
Hang upon his pent-house lid:
He shall live a man forbid:
Weary sev'nights, nine times nine,
Shall he dwindle, peak, and pine:
Though his bark cannot be lost,

Yet it shall be tempest-tost.
Look what I have.
SECOND WITCH: Show me, show me.
FIRST WITCH: Here I have a pilot's thumb,
Wrack'd, as homeward he did come.
Drum within.
THIRD WITCH: A drum, a drum:
Macbeth doth come.
ALL: The Weird Sisters, hand in hand,
Posters of the sea and land,
Thus do go, about, about,
Thrice to thine, and thrice to mine,
And thrice again, to make up nine.
Peace, the charm's wound up.
Enter Macbeth and Banquo.
MACBETH: So foul and fair a day I have not seen.
BANQUO: How far is't call'd to Forres? What are these,
So wither'd, and so wild in their attire,
That look not like th' inhabitants o' th' earth,
And yet are on't? Live you, or are you aught
That man may question? You seem to understand me,
By each at once her choppy finger laying
Upon her skinny lips: you should be women,
And yet your beards forbid me to interpret
That you are so.
MACBETH: Speak if you can: what are you?
FIRST WITCH: All hail Macbeth, hail to thee Thane of Glamis.
SECOND WITCH: All hail Macbeth, hail to thee Thane of Cawdor.
THIRD WITCH: All hail Macbeth, that shalt be King hereafter.
BANQUO: Good sir, why do you start, and seem to fear
Things that do sound so fair? I' th' name of truth
Are ye fantastical, or that indeed

Which outwardly ye show? My noble partner
You greet with present grace, and great prediction
Of noble having, and of royal hope,
That he seems rapt withal: to me you speak not.
If you can look into the seeds of Time,
And say, which grain will grow, and which will not,
Speak then to me, who neither beg, nor fear
Your favours, nor your hate.
FIRST WITCH: Hail.
SECOND WITCH: Hail.
THIRD WITCH: Hail.
FIRST WITCH: Lesser than Macbeth, and greater.
SECOND WITCH: Not so happy, yet much happier.
THIRD WITCH: Thou shalt get Kings, though thou be none:
So all hail Macbeth, and Banquo.
FIRST WITCH: Banquo, and Macbeth, all hail.
MACBETH: Stay you imperfect speakers, tell me more:
By Sinel's death, I know I am Thane of Glamis,
But how, of Cawdor? the Thane of Cawdor lives
A prosperous gentleman: and to be King,
Stands not within the prospect of belief,
No more than to be Cawdor. Say from whence
You owe this strange intelligence, or why
Upon this blasted Heath you stop our way
With such prophetic greeting?
Speak, I charge you.

Witches vanish.

BANQUO: The earth hath bubbles, as the water has,
And these are of them: whither are they vanish'd?
MACBETH: Into the air: and what seem'd corporal,
Melted, as breath into the wind.
Would they had stay'd.
BANQUO: Were such things here, as we do speak about?
Or have we eaten on the insane root,
That takes the reason prisoner?

MACBETH: Your children shall be Kings.
BANQUO: You shall be King.
MACBETH: And Thane of Cawdor too: went it not so?
BANQUO: To th' selfsame tune, and words: who's here?

Enter Ross and Angus.

ROSS: The King hath happily receiv'd, Macbeth,
The news of thy success: and when he reads
Thy personal venture in the rebels' fight,
His wonders and his praises do contend,
Which should be thine, or his: silenc'd with that,
In viewing o'er the rest o' th' selfsame day,
He finds thee in the stout Norweyan ranks,
Nothing afeard of what thyself didst make
Strange images of death. As thick as tale
Came post with post, and every one did bear
Thy praises in his Kingdom's great defence,
And pour'd them down before him.
ANGUS: We are sent,
To give thee from our Royal Master thanks,
Only to herald thee into his sight,
Not pay thee.
ROSS: And for an earnest of a greater honour,
He bade me, from him, call thee Thane of Cawdor:
In which addition, hail most worthy Thane,
For it is thine.
BANQUO: What, can the Devil speak true?
MACBETH: The Thane of Cawdor lives:
Why do you dress me in borrowed robes?
ANGUS : Who was the Thane, lives yet,
But under heavy judgement bears that life,
Which he deserves to lose.
Whether he was combin'd with those of Norway,
Or did line the rebel with hidden help,
And vantage; or that with both he labour'd
In his country's wrack, I know not:

But treasons capital, confess'd, and prov'd,
Have overthrown him.
MACBETH: Glamis, and Thane of Cawdor:
The greatest is behind. Thanks for your pains.
Do you not hope your children shall be Kings,
When those that gave the Thane of Cawdor to me,
Promis'd no less to them?
BANQUO: That trusted home,
Might yet enkindle you unto the Crown,
Besides the Thane of Cawdor. But 'tis strange:
And oftentimes, to win us to our harm,
The instruments of darkness tell us truths,
Win us with honest trifles, to betray's
In deepest consequence.
Cousins, a word, I pray you.
MACBETH: Two truths are told,
As happy Prologues to the swelling Act
Of the imperial theme. I thank you gentlemen:
This supernatural soliciting
Cannot be ill; cannot be good.
If ill? why hath it given me earnest of success,
Commencing in a truth? I am Thane of Cawdor.
If good? why do I yield to that suggestion,
Whose horrid image doth unfix my hair,
And make my seated heart knock at my ribs,
Against the use of Nature? Present fears
Are less than horrible imaginings:
My thought, whose murther yet is but fantastical,
Shakes so my single state of man,
That function is smother'd in surmise.
And nothing is, but what is not.
BANQUO: Look how our partner's rapt.
MACBETH: If Chance will have me King,
Why Chance may crown me,
Without my stir.

BANQUO: New honours come upon him
Like our strange garments, cleave not to their mould,
But with the aid of use.
MACBETH: Come what come may,
Time, and the hour, runs through the roughest day.
BANQUO: Worthy Macbeth, we stay upon your leisure.
MACBETH: Give me your favour:
My dull brain was wrought with things forgotten.
Kind gentlemen, your pains are register'd,
Where every day I turn the leaf,
To read them.
Let us toward the King: think upon
What hath chanc'd: and at more time,
The interim having weigh'd it, let us speak
Our free hearts each to other.
BANQUO: Very gladly.
MACBETH: Till then enough:
Come friends.

Exeunt.

I. 4

Flourish. Enter King Duncan, Lennox, Malcolm, Donalbain, and Attendants.

DUNCAN: Is execution done on Cawdor?
Are not those in commission yet return'd ?
MALCOLM: My Liege, they are not yet come back.
But I have spoke with one that saw him die:
Who did report, that very frankly he
Confess'd his treasons, implor'd you Highness' pardon.
And set forth a deep repentance:
Nothing in his life became him,
Like the leaving it. He died,
As one that had been studied in his death,

To throw away the dearest thing he ow'd.
As 'twere a careless trifle.
DUNCAN: There's no art,
To find the mind's construction in the face.
He was a gentleman, on whom I built
An absolute trust.

Enter Macbeth, Banquo, Ross, and Angus.

O worthiest cousin,
The sin of my ingratitude even now
Was heavy on me. Thou art so far before,
That swiftest wing of recompense is slow,
To overtake thee. Would thou hadst less deserv'd,
That the proportion both of thanks, and payment.
Might have been mine: only I have left to say,
More is thy due, than more than all can pay.
MACBETH: The service, and the loyalty I owe,
In doing it, pays itself.
Your Highness' part, is to receive our duties:
And our duties are to your throne, and state,
Children, and servants; which do but what they should.
By doing every thing safe toward your love
And honour.
DUNCAN : Welcome hither:
I have begun to plant thee, and will labour
To make thee full of growing. Noble Banquo,
That hast no less deserv'd, nor must be known
No less to have done so: let me enfold thee,
And hold thee to my heart.
BANQUO: There if I grow,
The harvest is your own.
DUNCAN: My plenteous joys,
Wanton in fulness, seek to hide themselves
In drops of sorrow. Sons, kinsmen, Thanes,
And you whose places are the nearest, know,
We will establish our estate upon

Our eldest, Malcolm, whom we name hereafter.
The Prince of Cumberland: which honour must
Not unaccompanied, invest him only,
But signs of nobleness, like stars, shall shine
On all deservers. From hence to Inverness,
And bind us further to you.

MACBETH: The rest is labour, which is not us'd for you:
I'll be myself the harbinger, and make joyful
The hearing of my wife, with your approach:
So humbly take my leave.

DUNCAN: My worthy Cawdor.

MACBETH : The Prince of Cumberland: that is a step,
On which I must fall down, or else o'erleap,
For in my way it lies. Stars hide your fires,
Let not light see my black and deep desires:
The eye wink at the hand; yet let that be,
Which the eye fears, when it is done to see.

Exit.

DUNCAN: True, worthy Banquo: he is full so valiant,
And in his commendations, I am fed:
It is a banquet to me. Let's after him,
Whose care is gone before, to bid us welcome:
It is a peerless kinsman.

Flourish. Exeunt.

I. 5

Enter Macbeth's wife alone with a letter.

LADY MACBETH: *They met me in the day of success: and I have learn'd by the perfect'st report, they have more in them, than mortal knowledge. When I burnt in desire to question them further, they made themselves air, into which they vanish'd. Whiles I stood rapt in the wonder of it, came missives from the King, who all-hail'd me Thane of Cawdor, by which title before, these Weird Sisters saluted me, and referr'd me to the coming on of time, with hail King that shalt be. This have I thought good to deliver thee (my dearest partner of greatness) that thou mightst not lose the dues of rejoicing by being ignorant of what greatness is promis'd thee. Lay it to thy heart and farewell.*

Glamis thou art, and Cawdor, and shalt be
What thou art promis'd: yet do I fear thy nature,
It is too full o' th' milk of humane kindness,
To catch the nearest way. Thou wouldst be great,
Art not without ambition, but without
The illness should attend it. What thou wouldst highly,
That wouldst thou holily: wouldst not play false,
And yet wouldst wrongly win.
Thou 'ldst have, great Glamis, that which cries,
Thus thou must do, if thou have it;
And that which rather thou dost fear to do,
Than wishest should be undone. Hie thee hither,
That I may pour my spirits in thine ear,
And chastise with the valour of my tongue
All that impedes thee from the golden round,
Which Fate and metaphysical aid doth seem
To have thee crown'd withal.

Enter Messenger.

What is your tidings?
MESSENGER: The King comes here to-night.
LADY MACBETH: Thou 'rt mad to say it.
Is not thy Master with him? who, were't so,
Would have inform'd for preparation.
MESSENGER: So please you, it is true: our Thane is coming:
One of my fellows had the speed of him;
Who almost dead for breath, had scarcely more
Than would make up his message.
LADY MACBETH: Give him tending,
He brings great news.

Exit Messenger.

The raven himself is hoarse,
That croaks the fatal entrance of Duncan
Under my battlements. Come you spirits,
That tend on mortal thoughts, unsex me here,
And fill me from the crown to the toe, top-full
Of direst cruelty: make thick my blood,
Stop up th' access and passage to remorse,
That no compunctious visitings of Nature
Shake my fell purpose, nor keep peace between
Th' effect, and it. Come to my woman's breasts,
And take my milk for gall, you murth'ring ministers.
Wherever, in your sightless substances,
You wait on Nature's mischief. Come thick Night,
And pall thee in the dunnest smoke of Hell,
That my keen knife see not the wound it makes,
Nor Heaven peep through the blanket of the dark,
To cry, hold, hold.

Enter Macbeth.

Great Glamis, worthy Cawdor,
Greater than both, by the all-hail hereafter,
Thy letters have transported me beyond
This ignorant present, and I feel now
The future in the instant.

MACBETH: My dearest love,
Duncan comes here to-night.

LADY MACBETH: And when goes hence?

MACBETH: To-morrow, as he purposes.

LADY MACBETH: O never,
Shall sun that morrow see.
Your face, my Thane, is as a book, where men
May read strange matters: to beguile the time,
Look like the time, bear welcome in your eye,
Your hand, your tongue: look like th' innocent flower,
But be the serpent under 't. He that's coming,
Must be provided for: and you shall put

This night's great business into my dispatch,
Which shall to all our nights, and days to come,
Give solely sovereign sway, and masterdom.
MACBETH: We will speak further.
LADY MACBETH: Only look up clear:
To alter favour, ever is to fear:
Leave all the rest to me.

Exeunt.

I. 6

Oboes, and torches, Enter King Duncan, Malcolm, Donalbain, Banquo, Lennox, Macduff, Ross, Angus, and Attendants.

DUNCAN: This Castle hath a pleasant seat,
The air nimbly and sweetly recommends itself
Unto our gentle senses.
BANQUO: This guest of summer,
The temple-haunting martlet does approve,
By this loved mansionry, that the Heaven's breath
Smells wooingly here: no jutty frieze,
Buttress, nor coign of vantage, but this bird
Hath made his pendent bed, and procreant cradle:
Where they most breed, and haunt, I have observ'd
The air is delicate.

Enter Lady Macbeth.

DUNCAN: See, see our honour'd hostess:
The love that follows us, sometime is our trouble,
Which still we thank as love. Herein I teach you,
How you shall bid God 'ild us for your pains,
And thank us for your trouble.
LADY MACBETH: All our service,
In every point twice done, and then done double,
Were poor, and single business, to contend
Against those honours deep, and broad,

Wherewith your Majesty loads our House:
For those of old, and the late dignities,
Heap'd up to them, we rest your hermits.
DUNCAN: Where's the Thane of Cawdor?
We cours'd him at the heels, and had a purpose
To be his purveyor: but he rides well,
And his great love (sharp as his spur) hath holp him
To his home before us: fair and noble hostess
We are your guest to-night.
LADY MACBETH: Your servants ever,
Have theirs, themselves, and what is theirs in compt,
To make their audit at your Highness' pleasure.
Still to return your own.
DUNCAN: Give me your hand:
Conduct me to mine host: we love him highly.
And shall continue our graces towards him.
By your leave hostess.

Exeunt.

I. 7

Oboes. Torches. Enter a Sewer, and divers Servants with dishes and service over the stage. Then enter Macbeth.

MACBETH: If it were done, when 'tis done, then 'twere well,
It were done quickly: if th' assassination
Could trammel up the consequence, and catch
With his surcease, success: that but this blow
Might be the be-all, and the end-all. Here,
But here, upon this bank and school of time,
We'ld jump the life to come. But in these cases,
We still have judgement here, that we but teach
Bloody instructions, which being taught, return
To plague th' inventor. This even-handed Justice

Commends th' ingredients of our poison'd chalice
To our own lips. He's here in double trust;
First, as I am his kinsman, and his subject,
Strong both against the deed: then, as his host,
Who should against his murtherer shut the door,
Not bear the knife myself. Besides, this Duncan
Hath borne his faculties so meek; hath been
So clear in his great office, that his virtues
Will plead like angels, trumpet-tongu'd against
The deep damnation of his taking-off:
And Pity, like a naked new-born babe,
Striding the blast, or Heaven's cherubin, hors'd
Upon the sightless couriers of the air,
Shall blow the horrid deed in every eye,
That tears shall drown the wind. I have no spur
To prick the sides of my intent, but only
Vaulting Ambition, which o'erleaps itself,
And falls on th' other.

Enter Lady Macbeth.

How now? What news?

LADY MACBETH: He has almost supp'd: why have you left the chamber?

MACBETH: Hath he ask'd for me?

LADY MACBETH: Know you not, he has?

MACBETH: We will proceed no further in this business:
He hath honour'd me of late, and I have bought
Golden opinions from all sorts of people,
Which would be worn now in their newest gloss,
Not cast aside so soon.

LADY MACBETH: Was the hope drunk,
Wherein you dress'd yourself? Hath it slept since?
And wakes it now to look so green, and pale,
At what it did so freely ? From this time,
Such I account thy love. Art thou afear'd
To be the same in thine own act, and valour,

As thou art in desire? Wouldst thou have that
Which thou esteem'st the ornament of life,
And live a coward in thine own esteem?
Letting I dare not, wait upon I would,
Like the poor cat i' th' adage.
MACBETH: Prithee peace:
I dare do all that may become a man,
Who dares do more, is none.
LADY MACBETH: What beast was't then
That made you break this enterprise to me?
When you durst do it, then you were a man:
And to be more than what you were, you would
Be so much more the man. Nor time, nor place
Did then adhere, and yet you would make both:
They have made themselves, and that their fitness now
Does unmake you. I have given suck, and know
How tender 'tis to love the babe that milks me:
I would, while it was smiling in my face,
Have pluck'd my nipple from his boneless gums,
And dash'd the brains out, had I so sworn
As you have done to this.
MACBETH: If we should fail?
LADY MACBETH: We fail?
But screw your courage to the sticking-place,
And we'll not fail: when Duncan is asleep,
(Whereto the rather shall his day's hard journey
Soundly invite him) his two chamberlains
Will I with wine, and wassail, so convince.
That memory, the warder of the brain,
Shall be a fume, and the receipt of reason
A limbeck only: when in swinish sleep,
Their drenched natures lie as in a death.
What cannot you and I perform upon
Th' unguarded Duncan? What not put upon
His spongy officers? who shall bear the guilt
Of our great quell.

MACBETH: Bring forth men-children only:
For thy undaunted mettle should compose
Nothing but males. Will it not be receiv'd,
When we have mark'd with blood those sleepy two
Of his own chamber, and us'd their very daggers,
That they have done't?
LADY MACBETH: Who dares receive it other,
As we shall make our griefs and clamour roar,
Upon his death?
MACBETH: I am settled, and bend up
Each corporal agent to this terrible feat.
Away, and mock the time with fairest show,
False face must hide what the false heart doth know.
Exeunt.

II. 1

Enter Banquo, and Fleance, with a torch before him.
BANQUO: How goes the night, boy ?
FLEANCE: The moon is down: I have not heard the clock.
BANQUO: And she goes down at twelve.
FLEANCE: I take't, 'tis later, sir.
BANQUO: Hold, take my sword:
There's husbandry in Heaven,
Their candles are all out: take thee that too.
A heavy summons lies like lead upon me,
And yet I would not sleep:
Powers, restrain in me the cursed thoughts
That Nature gives way to in repose.
Enter Macbeth, and a Servant with a torch.
Give me my sword: who's there?
MACBETH: A friend.
BANQUO: What sir, not yet at rest? The King's a-bed.

He hath been in unusual pleasure,
And sent forth great largess to your offices.
This diamond he greets your wife withal,
By the name of most kind hostess.
And shut up in measureless content.
MACBETH: Being unprepar'd,
Our will became the servant to defect,
Which else should free have wrought.
BANQUO: All's well.
I dreamt last night of the three Weird Sisters:
To you they have show'd some truth.
MACBETH: I think not of them:
Yet when we can entreat an hour to serve,
We would spend it in some words upon that business,
If you would grant the time.
BANQUO: At your kind'st leisure.
MACBETH: If you shall cleave to my consent,
When 'tis, it shall make honour for you.
BANQUO: So I lose none,
In seeking to augment it, but still keep
My bosom franchis'd, and allegiance clear,
I shall be counsell'd.
MACBETH: Good repose the while.
BANQUO: Thanks sir: the like to you.
Exeunt Banquo and Fleance.
MACBETH: Go bid thy Mistress, when my drink is ready,
She strike upon the bell. Get thee to bed.
Exit Servant.
Is this a dagger, which I see before me,
The handle toward my hand? Come, let me clutch thee:
I have thee not, and yet I see thee still.
Art thou not, fatal vision, sensible
To feeling, as to sight? or art thou but
A dagger of the mind, a false creation,
Proceeding from the heat-oppressed brain?

I see thee yet, in form as palpable,
As this which now I draw.
Thou marshall'st me the way that I was going,
And such an instrument I was to use.
Mine eyes are made the fools o' th' other senses,
Or else worth all the rest: I see thee still;
And on thy blade, and dudgeon, gouts of blood.
Which was not so before. There's no such thing:
It is the bloody business, which informs
Thus to mine eyes. Now o'er the one half-world
Nature seems dead, and wicked dreams abuse
The curtain'd sleep: witchcraft celebrates
Pale Hecat's offerings: and wither'd Murther,
Alarum'd by his sentinel, the wolf,
Whose howl's his watch, thus with his stealthy pace,
With Tarquin's ravishing strides, towards his design
Moves like a ghost. Thou sure and firm-set Earth
Hear not my steps, which way they walk, for fear
Thy very stones prate of my whereabout,
And take the present horror from the time,
Which now suits with it. Whiles I threat, he lives:
Words to the heat of deeds too cold breath gives.

A bell rings.

I go, and it is done: the bell invites me.
Hear it not, Duncan, for it is a knell,
That summons thee to Heaven, or to Hell.

Exit.

II. 2

Enter Lady Macbeth.

LADY MACBETH: That which hath made them drunk, hath made me bold:
What hath quench'd them, hath given me fire.

Hark, peace: it was the owl that shriek'd,
The fatal bellman, which gives the stern'st good-night.
He is about it, the doors are open:
And the surfeited grooms do mock their charge
With snores. I have drugg'd their possets,
That Death and Nature do contend about them,
Whether they live, or die.

Enter Macbeth.

MACBETH: Who's there? what hoa?
LADY MACBETH: Alack, I am afraid they have awak'd,
And 'tis not done: th' attempt, and not the deed,
Confounds us: hark: I laid their daggers ready,
He could not miss 'em. Had he not resembled
My father as he slept, I had done't.
My husband!
MACBETH: I have done the deed:
Didst thou not hear a noise?
LADY MACBETH: I heard the owl scream, and the crickets cry.
Did not you speak?
MACBETH: When?
LADY MACBETH : Now.
MACBETH: As I descended?
LADY MACBETH: Ay.
MACBETH: Hark, who lies i' th' second chamber?
LADY MACBETH: Donalbain.
MACBETH: This is a sorry sight.
LADY MACBETH: A foolish thought, to say a sorry sight.
MACBETH: There's one did laugh in's sleep,
And one cried Murther, that they did wake each other:
I stood, and heard them: but they did say their prayers,
And address'd them again to sleep.
LADY MACBETH: There are two lodg'd together.
MACBETH: One cried God bless us, and Amen the other,
As they had seen me with these hangman's hands:
Listening their fear, I could not say Amen,

When they did say God bless us.
LADY MACBETH: Consider it not so deeply.
MACBETH: But wherefore could not I pronounce Amen?
I had most need of blessing, and Amen stuck in my throat.
LADY MACBETH: These deeds must not be thought
After these ways: so, it will make us mad.
MACBETH : Methought I heard a voice cry, Sleep no more:
Macbeth does murther Sleep, the innocent Sleep,
Sleep that knits up the ravell'd sleave of care,
The death of each day's life, sore labour's bath,
Balm of hurt minds, great Nature's second course,
Chief nourisher in Life's feast.
LADY MACBETH: What do you mean?
MACBETH: Still it cri'd, Sleep no more to all the House:
Glamis hath murther'd Sleep, and therefore Cawdor
Shall sleep no more: Macbeth shall sleep no more.
LADY MACBETH: Who was it, that thus cried? Why worthy Thane,
You do unbend your noble strength, to think
So brain-sickly of things: go get some water,
And wash this filthy witness from your hand.
Why did you bring these daggers from the place?
They must lie there: go carry them, and smear
The sleepy grooms with blood.
MACBETH: I'll go no more:
I am afraid, to think what I have done:
Look on't again, I dare not.
LADY MACBETH: Infirm of purpose:
Give me the daggers: the sleeping, and the dead,
Are but as pictures: 'tis the eye of childhood,
That fears a painted devil. If he do bleed,
I'll gild the faces of the grooms withal,
For it must seem their guilt.

Exit. Knock within.

MACBETH: Whence is that knocking?
How is't with me, when every noise appals me?
What hands are here? hah : they pluck out mine eyes.
Will all great Neptune's Ocean wash this blood
Clean from my hand? No: this my hand will rather
The multitudinous seas incarnadine,
Making the green one, red.

Enter Lady Macbeth.

LADY MACBETH: My hands are of your colour: but I shame
To wear a heart so white.

Knock.

I hear a knocking at the south entry:
Retire we to our chamber:
A little water clears us of this deed.
How easy is it then? Your constancy
Hath left you unattended.

Knock.

Hark, more knocking.
Get on your nightgown, lest occasion call us,
And show us to be watchers: be not lost
So poorly in your thoughts.

MACBETH: To know my deed,

Knock.

'Twere best not know myself.
Wake Duncan with thy knocking:
I would thou could'st.

Exeunt.

II. 3

Enter a Porter. Knocking within.

PORTER: Here's a knocking indeed: if a man were Porter of Hell Gate, he should have old turning the key. (*Knock.*) Knock, knock, knock. Who's there i' th' name of Beelzebub? Here's a farmer, that hang'd himself on th' expectation of plenty: come in time, have napkins enow about you, here you'll sweat for't. (*Knock.*) Knock, knock. Who's there in th' other Devil's name? Faith here's an equivocator, that could swear in both the scales against either scale, who committed treason enough for God's sake, yet could not equivocate to Heaven: oh come in, equivocator. (*Knock.*) Knock, knock, knock. Who's there? 'Faith here's an English tailor come hither, for stealing out of a French hose: come in tailor, here you may roast your goose. (*Knock.*) Knock, knock. Never at quiet: what are you? But this place is too cold for Hell. I'll devil-porter it no further: I had thought to have let in some of all professions, that go the primrose way to th' everlasting bonfire. (*Knock.*) Anon, anon, I pray you remember the porter.

Enter Macduff, and Lennox.

MACDUFF: Was it so late, friend, ere you went to bed,
That you do lie so late?

PORTER : 'Faith sir, we were carousing till the second cock: and drink sir, is a great provoker of three things.

MACDUFF: What three things does drink especially provoke?

PORTER: Marry, sir, nose-painting, sleep, and urine. Lechery, sir, it provokes and unprovokes: it provokes the desire, but it takes away the performance. Therefore much drink may be said to be an equivocator with lechery: it makes him, and it mars him; it sets him on, and it takes him off; it persuades him, and disheartens him; makes him stand to, and not stand to: in conclusion, equivocates him in a sleep, and, giving him the lie, leaves him.

MACDUFF: I believe, drink gave thee the lie last night.

PORTER: That it did, sir, i' the very throat on me: but I requited him for his lie, and (I think) being too strong for him, though he took up my legs sometime, yet I made a shift to cast him.

Enter Macbeth.

MACDUFF: Is thy Master stirring?
Our knocking has awak'd him: here he comes.

LENNOX: Good morrow, noble sir.
MACBETH: Good morrow both.
MACDUFF: Is the King stirring, worthy Thane?
MACBETH: Not yet.
MACDUFF: He did command me to call timely on him;
I have almost slipp'd the hour.
MACBETH: I'll bring you to him.
MACDUFF: I know this is a joyful trouble to you:
But yet 'tis one.
MACBETH: The labour we delight in, physics pain:
This is the door.
MACDUFF: I'll make so bold to call, for 'tis my limited service.

Exit Macduff.

LENNOX: Goes the King hence to-day?
MACBETH: He does: he did appoint so.
LENNOX: The night has been unruly:
Where we lay, our chimneys were blown down,
And (as they say) lamentings heard i' th' air;
Strange screams of death,
And prophesying, with accents terrible.
Of dire combustion, and confus'd events,
New hatch'd to th' woeful time.
The obscure bird clamour'd the livelong night.
Some say, the earth was feverous,
And did shake.
MACBETH: 'Twas a rough night.
LENNOX : My young remembrance cannot parallel
A fellow to it.

Enter Macduff.

MACDUFF: O horror, horror, horror,
Tongue nor heart cannot conceive, nor name thee.
MACBETH AND LENNOX: What's the matter?
MACDUFF: Confusion now hath made his masterpiece:
Most sacrilegious murther hath broke ope

The Lord's anointed Temple, and stole thence
The life o' th' building.
MACBETH: What is't you say, the life?
LENNOX: Mean you his Majesty?
MACDUFF: Approach the chamber, and destroy your sight
With a new Gorgon. Do not bid me speak :
See, and then speak yourselves: awake, awake,
Exeunt Macbeth and Lennox.
Ring the alarum-bell: murther, and treason,
Banquo, and Donalbain: Malcolm awake.
Shake off this downy sleep, Death's counterfeit,
And look on Death itself: up, up, and see
The great Doom's image: Malcolm, Banquo,
As from your graves rise up, and walk like sprites,
To countenance this horror. Ring the bell
Bell rings. Enter Lady Macbeth.
LADY MACBETH: What's the business?
That such a hideous trumpet calls to parley
The sleepers of the House? speak, speak.
MACDUFF: O gentle Lady,
'Tis not for you to hear what I can speak:
The repetition in a woman's ear,
Would murther as it fell.
Enter Banquo.
O Banquo, Banquo, our Royal Master's murther'd.
LADY MACBETH: Woe, alas:
What, in our House?
BANQUO: Too cruel, any where.
Dear Duff, I prithee contradict thyself,
And say, it is not so.
Enter Macbeth, Lennox and Ross.
MACBETH: Had I but died an hour before this chance,
I had liv'd a blessed time: for from this instant,
There's nothing serious in mortality:
All is but toys: Renown and Grace is dead,

The wine of Life is drawn, and the mere lees.
Is left this vault, to brag of.
Enter Malcolm and Donalbain.
DONALBAIN: What is amiss?
MACBETH: You are, and do not know't:
The spring, the head, the fountain of your blood
Is stopp'd, the very source of it is stopp'd.
MACDUFF: Your Royal Father's murther'd
MALCOLM: O, by whom ?
LENNOX: Those of his chamber, as it seem'd, had done't:
Their hands and faces were all badg'd with blood,
So were their daggers, which unwip'd, we found
Upon their pillows: they star'd, and were distracted,
No man's life was to be trusted with them.
MACBETH: O, yet I do repent me of my fury,
That I did kill them.
MACDUFF: Wherefore did you so?
MACBETH: Who can be wise, amaz'd, temperate, and furious.
Loyal, and neutral, in a moment? No man :
Th' expedition of my violent love
Outrun the pauser, Reason. Here lay Duncan,
His silver skin, lac'd with his golden blood,
And his gash'd stabs, look'd like a breach in Nature,
For Ruin's wasteful entrance: there the murtherers,
Steep'd in the colours of their trade; their daggers
Unmannerly breech'd with gore: who could refrain,
That had a heart to love; and in that heart
Courage, to make's love known?
LADY MACBETH: Help me hence, hoa.
MACDUFF: Look to the Lady.
MALCOLM: Why do we hold our tongues,
That most may claim this argument for ours?
DONALBAIN: What should be spoken here,
Where our fate hid in an auger-hole,
May rush, and seize us? Let's away,

Our tears are not yet brew'd.
MALCOLM: Nor our strong sorrow
Upon the foot of motion.
BANQUO: Look to the Lady:
And when we have our naked frailties hid,
That suffer in exposure, let us meet,
And question this most bloody piece of work,
To know it further. Fears and scruples shake us:
In the great hand of God I stand, and thence,
Against the indivulg'd pretence, I fight
Of treasonous malice.
MACDUFF: And so do I.
ALL: So all.
MACBETH: Let's briefly put on manly readiness,
And meet i' th' Hall together.
ALL: Well contented.

Exeunt.

MALCOLM: What will you do?
Let's not consort with them:
To show an unfelt sorrow, is an office
Which the false man does easy.
I'll to England.
DONALBAIN: To Ireland I:
Our separated fortune shall keep us both the safer:
Where we are, there's daggers in men's smiles;
The near in blood, the nearer bloody.
MALCOLM: This murtherous shaft that's shot,
Hath not yet lighted: and our safest way,
Is to avoid the aim. Therefore to horse,
And let us not be dainty of leave-taking,
But shift away: there's warrant in that theft,
Which steals itself, when there's no mercy left.

Exeunt.

II. 4

Enter Ross, with an old Man.

OLD MAN: Threescore and ten I can remember well,
Within the volume of which time, I have seen
Hours dreadful, and things strange: but this sore night
Hath trifled former knowings.

ROSS: Ha, good father,
Thou seest the Heavens, as troubled with man's act,
Threatens his bloody stage: by th' clock 'tis day,
And yet dark Night strangles the travelling lamp:
Is't Night's predominance, or the Day's shame,
That Darkness does the face of Earth entomb,
When living Light should kiss it?

OLD MAN: 'Tis unnatural,
Even like the deed that's done: on Tuesday last,
A falcon towering in her pride of place,
Was by a mousing owl hawk'd at, and kill'd.

ROSS: And Duncan's horses.
(A thing most strange and certain)
Beauteous, and swift, the minions of their race,
Turn'd wild in nature, broke their stalls, flung out,
Contending 'gainst obedience, as they would
Make war with mankind.

OLD MAN: 'Tis said, they eat each other.

ROSS: They did so:
To th' amazement of mine eyes that look'd upon't.

Enter Macduff.

Here comes the good Macduff.
How goes the world sir, now?

MACDUFF: Why see you not?

ROSS: Is't known who did this more than bloody deed?

MACDUFF: Those that Macbeth hath slain,

ROSS: Alas the day,
What good could they pretend?

MACDUFF: They were suborned :
Malcolm and Donalbain, the King's two sons,
Are stol'n away and fled, which puts upon them
Suspicion of the deed.
ROSS: 'Gainst Nature still;
Thriftless Ambition, that wilt ravin up
Thine own life's means: then 'tis most like,
The sovereignty will fall upon Macbeth.
MACDUFF: He is already nam'd, and gone to Scone
To be invested.
ROSS: Where is Duncan's body?
MACDUFF: Carried to Colmekill,
The sacred storehouse of his predecessors,
And guardian of their bones.
ROSS: Will you to Scone?
MACDUFF: No cousin, I'll to Fife.
ROSS : Well, I will thither.
MACDUFF: Well may you see things well done there: adieu,
Lest our old robes sit easier than our new.
ROSS: Farewell, father.
OLD MAN: God's benison go with you, and with those
That would make good of bad, and friends of foes.

Exeunt omnes.

III. 1

Enter Banquo.

BANQUO: Thou hast it now, King, Cawdor, Glamis, all.
As the Weird Women promis'd, and I fear
Thou play'dst most foully for't: yet it was said
It should not stand in thy posterity,
But that myself should be the root, and father
Of many Kings. If there come truth from them,
As upon thee Macbeth, their speeches shine,

Why by the verities on thee made good,
May they not be my oracles as well,
And set me up in hope? But hush, no more.

Sennet sounded. Enter Macbeth as King, Lady Macbeth, Lennox, Ross, Lords, and Attendants.

MACBETH: Here's our chief guest.
LADY MACBETH: If he had been forgotten,
It had been as a gap in our great feast,
And all-thing unbecoming.
MACBETH: To-night we hold a solemn supper sir,
And I'll request your presence.
BANQUO : Let your Highness
Command upon me, to the which my duties
Are with a most indissoluble tie
For ever knit.
MACBETH: Ride you this afternoon?
BANQUO: Ay, my good Lord.
MACBETH : We should have else desir'd your good advice
(Which still hath been both grave, and prosperous)
In this day's Council: but we'll take to-morrow.
Is't far you ride?
BANQUO: As far, my Lord, as will fill up the time
'Twixt this, and supper. Go not my horse the better,
I must become a borrower of the night,
For a dark hour, or twain.
MACBETH: Fail not our feast.
BANQUO: My Lord, I will not.
MACBETH: We hear our bloody cousins are bestow'd
In England, and in Ireland, not confessing
Their cruel parricide, filling their hearers
With strange invention. But of that to-morrow,
When therewithal, we shall have cause of state,
Craving us jointly. Hie you to horse:
Adieu, till you return at night.
Goes Fleance with you?

BANQUO: Ay, my good Lord: our time does call upon's.
MACBETH: I wish your horses swift, and sure of foot:
And so I do commend you to their backs.
Farewell.

Exit Banquo.

Let every man be master of his time,
Till seven at night, to make society
The sweeter welcome:
We will keep ourself till supper-time alone:
While then, God be with you.

Exeunt all but Macbeth, and a servant.

Sirrah, a word with you: attend those men
Our pleasure?
SERVANT: They are, my Lord, without the Palace Gate.
MACBETH: Bring them before us.

Exit Servant.

To be thus, is nothing, but to be safely thus.
Our fears in Banquo stick deep,
And in his royalty of Nature reigns that
Which would be fear'd. 'Tis much he dares,
And to that dauntless temper of his mind,
He hath a wisdom, that doth guide his valour,
To act in safety. There is none but he,
Whose being I do fear: and under him,
My Genius is rebuk'd, as it is said
Mark Antony's was by Caesar. He chid the Sisters,
When first they put the name of King upon me,
And bad them speak to him. Then prophet-like,
They hail'd him father to a line of Kings.
Upon my head they plac'd a fruitless crown,
And put a barren sceptre in my gripe,
Thence to be wrench'd with an unlineal hand,
No son of mine succeeding: if't be so,
For Banquo's issue have I fil'd my mind,
For them, the gracious Duncan have 1 murther'd,

Put rancours in the vessel of my peace
Only for them, and mine eternal jewel
Given to the common Enemy of man,
To make them Kings, the seeds of Banquo Kings.
Rather than so, come Fate into the list,
And champion me to th' utterance.
Who's there;

Enter Servant, and two Murtherers.

Now go to the door, and stay there till we call.

Exit Servant.

Was it not yesterday we spoke together?

FIRST MURDERER: It was, so please your Highness.

MACBETH: Well then,
Now have you consider'd of my speeches:
Know, that it was he, in the times past,
Which held you so under fortune,
Which, you thought had been our innocent self.
This I made good to you, in our last conference,
Pass'd in probation with you :
How you were borne in hand, how cross'd:
The instruments: who wrought with them:
And all things else, that might
To half a soul, and to a notion craz'd.
Say, Thus did Banquo.

FIRST MURDERER: You made it known to us.

MACBETH: I did so:
And went further, which is now
Our point of second meeting.
Do you find your patience so predominant,
In your nature, that you can let this go?
Are you so gospell'd, to pray for this good man,
And for his issue, whose heavy hand
Hath bow'd you to the grave, and beggar'd
Yours for ever?

FIRST MURDERER: We are men, my Liege.

MACBETH: Ay, in the catalogue ye go for men,
As hounds, and greyhounds, mongrels, spaniels, curs,
Shoughs, water-rugs, and demi-wolves are clept
All by the name of dogs: the valued file
Distinguishes the swift, the slow, the subtle,
The housekeeper, the hunter, every one
According to the gift, which bounteous Nature
Hath in him clos'd: whereby he does receive
Particular addition, from the bill,
That writes them all alike: and so of men.
Now, if you have a station in the file,
Not i' th' worst rank of manhood, say't,
And I will put that business in your bosoms,
Whose execution takes your enemy off,
Grapples you to the heart, and love of us,
Who wear our health but sickly in his life,
Which in his death were perfect.
SECOND MURDERER: I am one, my Liege,
Whom the vile blows and buffets of the world
Hath so incens'd, that I am reckless what I do,
To spite the world.
FIRST MURDERER: And I another,
So weary with disasters, tugg'd with Fortune,
That I would set my life on any chance,
To mend it, or be rid on't.
MACBETH: Both of you know Banquo was your enemy.
BOTH MURDERERS: True, my Lord.
MACBETH: So is he mine: and in such bloody distance,
That every minute of his being, thrusts
Against my near'st of life: and though I could
With barefac'd power sweep him from my sight,
And bid my will avouch it; yet I must not,
For certain friends that are both his, and mine,
Whose loves I may not drop, but wail his fall,
Who I myself struck down: and thence it is,

That I to your assistance do make love,
Masking the business from the common eye,
For sundry weighty reasons.
SECOND MURDERER : We shall, my Lord,
Perform what you command us.
FIRST MURDERER: Though our lives—
MACBETH: Your spirits shine through you.
Within this hour, at most,
I will advise you where to plant yourselves,
Acquaint you with the perfect spy o' th' time,
The moment on't, for't must be done to-night,
And something from the Palace: always thought,
That I require a clearness; and with him,
To leave no rubs nor botches in the work,
Fleance, his son, that keeps him company,
Whose absence is no less material to me,
Than is his father's, must embrace the fate
Of that dark hour: resolve yourselves apart,
I'll come to you anon.
BOTH MURDERERS: We are resolv'd, my Lord.
MACBETH: I'll call upon you straight: abide within,
It is concluded: Banquo, thy soul's flight,
If it find Heaven, must find it out to-night.

Exeunt.

III. 2

Enter Lady Macbeth, and a Servant.

LADY MACBETH: Is Banquo gone from Court?
SERVANT: Ay, Madam, but returns again to-night.
LADY MACBETH: Say to the King, I would attend his leisure,
For a few words.
SERVANT: Madam, I will.

Exit.

LADY MACBETH: Nought's had, all's spent,
Where our desire is got without content:
'Tis safer, to be that which we destroy,
Than by destruction dwell in doubtful joy.

Enter Macbeth.

How now, my Lord, why do you keep alone?
Of sorriest fancies your companions making,
Using those thoughts, which should indeed have died
With them they think on: things without all remedy
Should be without regard: what's done, is done.

MACBETH : We have scorch'd the snake, not kill'd it:
She'll close, and be herself, whilst our poor malice
Remains in danger of her former tooth.
But let the frame of things disjoint,
Both the worlds suffer,
Ere we will eat our meal in fear, and sleep
In the affliction of these terrible dreams,
That shake us nightly: better be with the dead,
Whom we, to gain our peace, have sent to peace,
Than on the torture of the mind to lie
In restless ecstasy.
Duncan is in his grave;
After life's fitful fever, he sleeps well,
Treason has done his worst: nor steel, nor poison,
Malice domestic, foreign levy, nothing,
Can touch him further.

LADY MACBETH: Come on:
Gentle my Lord, sleek o'er your rugged looks,
Be bright and jovial among your guests to-night.

MACBETH: So shall I Love, and so I pray be you:
Let your remembrance apply to Banquo,
Present him eminence, both with eye and tongue:
Unsafe the while, that we must lave
Our honours in these flattering streams,
And make our faces vizards to our hearts,

Disguising what they are.
LADY MACBETH: You must leave this.
MACBETH: O, full of scorpions is my mind, dear wife:
Thou know'st, that Banquo and his Fleance lives.
LADY MACBETH : But in them, Nature's copy's not eterne.
MACBETH: There's comfort yet, they are assailable,
Then be thou jocund: ere the bat hath flown
His cloister'd flight, ere to black Hecat's summons
The shard-borne beetle, with his drowsy hums,
Hath rung night's yawning peal,
There shall be done a deed of dreadful note.
LADY MACBETH: What's to be done?
MACBETH: Be innocent of the knowledge, dearest chuck,
Till thou applaud the deed: come, seeling Night,
Scarf up the tender eye of pitiful Day,
And with thy bloody and invisible hand
Cancel and tear to pieces that great bond,
Which keeps me pale. Light thickens,
And the crow makes wing to th' rooky wood:
Good things of Day begin to droop, and drowse,
Whiles Night's black agents to their preys do rouse.
Thou marvell'st at my words: but hold thee still,
Things bad begun, make strong themselves by ill:
So prithee go with me.

Exeunt.

III. 3

Enter three Murtherers.

FIRST MURDERER: But who did bid thee join with us?
THIRD MURDERER: Macbeth.
SECOND MURDERER: He needs not our mistrust, since he delivers
Our offices, and what we have to do,

To the direction just.

FIRST MURDERER: Then stand with us:
The West yet glimmers with some streaks of day.
Now spurs the lated traveller apace,
To gain the timely inn, and near approaches
The subject of our watch.

THIRD MURDERER: Hark, I hear horses.

BANQUO (*within*): Give us a light there, hoa.

SECOND MURDERER: Then 'tis he:
The rest, that are within the note of expectation.
Already are i' th' Court.

FIRST MURDERER: His horses go about.

THIRD MURDERER: Almost a mile: but he does usually.
So all men do, from hence to th' Palace Gate
Make it their walk.

Enter Banquo, and Fleance, with a torch.

SECOND MURDERER: A light, a light.

THIRD MURDERER: 'Tis he.

FIRST MURDERER: Stand to't.

BANQUO: It will be rain to-night.

FIRST MURDERER: Let it come down.

BANQUO: O, treachery!
Fly good Fleance, fly, fly, fly.
Thou mayst revenge. O slave!

THIRD MURDERER: Who did strike out the light?

FIRST MURDERER: Was't not the way?

THIRD MURDERER: There's but one down: the son is fled.

SECOND MURDERER: We have lost
Best half of our affair.

FIRST MURDERER: Well, let's away, and say how much is done.

Exeunt.

III. 4

Banquet prepared. Enter Macbeth, Lady Macbeth, Ross, Lennox, Lords, and Attendants.

MACBETH: You know your own degrees, sit down:
At first and last, the hearty welcome.
LORDS: Thanks to your Majesty.
MACBETH: Ourself will mingle with society,
And play the humble host:
Our hostess keeps her state, but in best time
We will require her welcome.
LADY MACBETH: Pronounce it for me sir, to all our friends,
For my heart speaks, they are welcome.

Enter First Murtherer.

MACBETH: See they encounter thee with their hearts' thanks,
Both sides are even: here I'll sit i' th' midst,
Be large in mirth, anon we'll drink a measure
The table round. There's blood upon thy face.
MURDERER: 'Tis Banquo's then.
MACBETH: 'Tis better thee without, than he within.
Is he dispatch'd?
MURDERER : My Lord his throat is cut, that I did for him.
MACBETH: Thou art the best o' th' cut-throats.
Yet he's good that did the like for Fleance.
If thou didst it, thou art the nonpareil.
MURDERER: Most Royal Sir,
Fleance is 'scap'd.
MACBETH: Then comes my fit again:
I had else been perfect;
Whole as the marble, founded as the rock,
As broad, and general, as the casing air:
But now I am cabin'd, cribb'd, confin'd, bound in
To saucy doubts, and fears. But Banquo's safe?
MURDERER: Ay, my good Lord: safe in a ditch he bides,

With twenty trenched gashes on his head;
The least a death to Nature.

MACBETH: Thanks for that:
There the grown serpent lies, the worm that's fled
Hath nature that in time will venom breed.
No teeth for th' present. Get thee gone, to-morrow
We'll hear ourselves again.

Exit Murderer.

LADY MACBETH: My Royal Lord,
You do not give the cheer: the feast is sold
That is not often vouch'd, while 'tis a-making ,
'Tis given, with welcome: to feed were best at home:
From thence, the sauce to meat is ceremony,
Meeting were bare without it.

Enter the Ghost of Banquo, and sits in Macbeth's place.

MACBETH: Sweet remembrancer:
Now good digestion wait on appetite.
And health on both.

LENNOX: May't please your Highness sit.

MACBETH: Here had we now our country's honour, roof'd,
Were the grac'd person of our Banquo present:
Who, may I rather challenge for unkindness,
Than pity for mischance.

ROSS: His absence, Sir,
Lays blame upon his promise. Please't your Highness
To grace us with your royal company?

MACBETH: The table's full.

LENNOX: Here is a place reserv'd Sir.

MACBETH: Where?

LENNOX: Here my good Lord.
What is't that moves your Highness?

MACBETH: Which of you have done this?

LORDS: What, my good Lord?

MACBETH: Thou canst not say I did it: never shake
Thy gory locks at me.

ROSS: Gentlemen rise, his Highness is not well.
LADY MACBETH: Sit worthy friends: my Lord is often thus,
And hath been from his youth. Pray you keep seat,
The fit is momentary, upon a thought
He will again be well. If much you note him,
You shall offend him, and extend his passion,
Feed, and regard him not. Are you a man?
MACBETH: Ay, and a bold one, that dare look on that
Which might appal the Devil.
LADY MACBETH: O proper stuff:
This is the very painting of your fear:
This is the air-drawn dagger which you said
Led you to Duncan. O, these flaws and starts
(Impostors to true fear) would well become
A woman's story, at a winter's fire
Authoriz'd by her grandam: shame itself,
Why do you make such faces? When all's done
You look but on a stool.
MACBETH: Prithee see there:
Behold, look, lo, how say you?
Why what care I, if thou canst nod, speak too.
If charnel-houses, and our graves must send
Those that we bury, back; our monuments
Shall be the maws of kites.

Exit Ghost.

LADY MACBETH: What? quite unmann'd in folly.
MACBETH : If I stand here, I saw him.
LADY MACBETH: Fie for shame.
MACBETH: Blood hath been shed ere now, i' th' olden time
Ere humane statute purg'd the gentle weal:
Ay, and since too, murthers have been perform'd
Too terrible for the ear. The time has been,
That when the brains were out, the man would die,
And there an end: but now they rise again

With twenty mortal murthers on their crowns,
And push us from our stools. This is more strange
Than such a murther is.

LADY MACBETH: My worthy Lord
Your noble friends do lack you.

MACBETH : I do forget:
Do not muse at me my most worthy friends,
I have a strange infirmity, which is nothing
To those that know me. Come, love and health to all,
Then I'll sit down: give me some wine, fill full.

Enter Ghost.

I drink to th' general joy o' th' whole table,
And to our dear friend Banquo, whom we miss:
Would he were here: to all, and him we thirst,
And all to all.

LORDS: Our duties, and the pledge.

MACBETH: Avaunt, and quit my sight, let the earth hide thee:
Thy bones are marrowless, thy blood is cold:
Thou hast no speculation in those eyes
Which thou dost glare with.

LADY MACBETH: Think of this good Peers
But as a thing of custom: 'tis no other,
Only it spoils the pleasure of the time.

MACBETH: What man dare, I dare:
Approach thou like the rugged Russian bear,
The arm'd rhinoceros, or th' Hyrcan tiger,
Take any shape but that, and my firm nerves
Shall never tremble. Or be alive again,
And dare me to the desert with thy sword:
If trembling I inhabit then, protest me
The baby of a girl. Hence horrible shadow,
Unreal mockery hence.

Exit Ghost.

Why so, being gone

I am a man again: pray you sit still.
LADY MACBETH: You have displac'd the mirth,
Broke the good meeting, with most admir'd disorder.
MACBETH: Can such things be,
And overcome us like a summer's cloud,
Without our special wonder? You make me strange
Even to the disposition that I owe,
When now I think you can behold such sights,
And keep the natural ruby of your cheeks,
When mine is blanch'd with fear.
ROSS : What sights my Lord?
LADY MACBETH: I pray you speak not: he grows worse and worse:
Question enrages him: at once, good night.
Stand not upon the order of your going,
But go at once.
LENNOX: Good night, and better health
Attend his Majesty.
LADY MACBETH: A kind good night to all.
Exit Lords.
MACBETH: It will have blood they say:
Blood will have blood:
Stones have been known to move, and trees to speak:
Augurs, and understood relations, have
By magot-pies, and choughs, and rooks brought forth
The secret'st man of blood. What is the night?
LADY MACBETH: Almost at odds with morning, which is which.
MACBETH: How say'st thou that Macduff denies his person
At our great bidding?
LADY MACBETH : Did you send to him Sir?
MACBETH: I hear it by the way: but I will send:
There's not a one of them but in his house
I keep a servant feed. I will to-morrow
(And betimes I will) to the Weird Sisters.

More shall they speak: for now I am bent to know
By the worst means, the worst; for mine own good,
All causes shall give way. I am in blood
Stepp'd in so far, that should I wade no more,
Returning were as tedious as go o'er:
Strange things I have in head, that will to hand,
Which must be acted, ere they may be scann'd.
LADY MACBETH: You lack the season of all natures, sleep.
MACBETH: Come, we'll to sleep: my strange and self-abuse
Is the initiate fear, that wants hard use:
We are yet but young in deed.
Exeunt.

III. 5

Thunder. Enter the three Witches, meeting Hecat.
FIRST WITCH: Why how now Hecat, you look angerly?
HECAT : Have I not reason, beldams as you are?
Saucy, and overbold, how did you dare
To trade, and traffic with Macbeth,
In riddles, and affairs of death;
And I the mistress of your charms,
The close contriver of all harms,
Was never call'd to bear my part,
Or show the glory of our art?
And which is worse, all you have done
Hath been but for a wayward son,
Spiteful, and wrathful, who (as others do)
Loves for his own ends, not for you.
But make amends now: get you gone,
And at the pit of Acheron
Meet me i' th' morning: thither he
Will come, to know his destiny.
Your vessels, and your spells provide,

Your charms, and every thing beside;
I am for th' air: this night I'll spend
Unto a dismal, and a fatal end.
Great business must be wrought ere noon.
Upon the corner of the moon
There hangs a vaporous drop, profound,
I'll catch it ere it come to ground;
And that distill'd by magic sleights,
Shall raise such artificial sprites,
As by the strength of their illusion,
Shall draw him on to his confusion.
He shall spurn Fate, scorn Death, and bear
His hopes 'bove wisdom, grace, and fear:
And you all know, security
Is mortals' chiefest enemy.

Music, and a song.

Hark, I am call'd: my little spirit see,
Sits in a foggy cloud, and stays for me.

Song within 'Come away, come away,' etc.

FIRST WITCH: Come, let's make haste, she'll soon be
Back again.

Exeunt.

III. 6

Enter Lennox, and another Lord.

LENNOX : My former speeches,
Have but hit your thoughts
Which can interpret farther: only I say
Things have been strangely borne. The gracious Duncan
Was pitied of Macbeth: marry he was dead:
And the right valiant Banquo walk'd too late,
Whom you may say (if't please you) Fleance kill'd,
For Fleance fled: men must not walk too late.

Who cannot want the thought, how monstrous
It was for Malcolm, and for Donalbain
To kill their gracious father? Damned fact,
How it did grieve Macbeth! Did he not straight
In pious rage, the two delinquents tear,
That were the slaves of drink, and thralls of sleep?
Was not that nobly done? Ay, and wisely too:
For 'twould have anger'd any heart alive
To hear the men deny't. So that I say,
He has borne all things well, and I do think,
That had he Duncan's sons under his key,
(As, and't please Heaven he shall not) they should find
What 'twere to kill a father: so should Fleance.
But peace; for from broad words, and 'cause he fail'd
His presence at the tyrant's feast, I hear
Macduff lives in disgrace. Sir, can you tell
Where he bestows himself?
LORD: The son of Duncan
(From whom this tyrant holds the due of birth)
Lives in the English Court, and is receiv'd
Of the most pious Edward, with such grace,
That the malevolence of Fortune nothing
Takes from his high respect. Thither Macduff
Is gone, to pray the holy King, upon his aid
To wake Northumberland, and warlike Siward,
That by the help of these (with Him above
To ratify the work) we may again
Give to our tables meat, sleep to our nights:
Free from our feasts, and banquets bloody knives;
Do faithful homage, and receive free honours,
All which we pine for now. And this report
Hath so exasperate the King, that he
Prepares for some attempt of war.
LENNOX: Sent he to Macduff?
LORD: He did: and with an absolute Sir, not I

The cloudy messenger turns me his back,
And hums; as who should say, you'll rue the time
That clogs me with this answer.
LENNOX: And that well might
Advise him to a caution, to hold what distance
His wisdom can provide. Some holy Angel
Fly to the Court of England, and unfold
His message ere he come, that a swift blessing
May soon return to this our suffering country.
Under a hand accurs'd.
LORD : I'll send my prayers with him.

Exeunt.

IV. 1

Thunder. Enter the three Witches.

FIRST WITCH: Thrice the brinded cat hath mew'd.
SECOND WITCH: Thrice, and once the hedge-pig whin'd
THIRD WITCH: Harpier cries, 'tis time, 'tis time.
FIRST WITCH: Round about the cauldron go:
In the poison'd entrails throw.
Toad, that under cold stone,
Days and nights, has thirty one:
Swelter'd venom sleeping got,
Boil thou first i' th' charmed pot.
ALL: Double, double, toil and trouble;
Fire burn, and cauldron bubble.
SECOND WITCH: Fillet of a fenny snake,
In the cauldron boil and bake:
Eye of newt, and toe of frog,
Wool of bat, and tongue of dog:
Adder's fork, and blind-worm's sting,
Lizard's leg, and howlet's wing:
For a charm of powerful trouble,

Like a hell-broth, boil and bubble.
ALL: Double, double, toil and trouble,
Fire burn, and cauldron bubble.
THIRD WITCH: Scale of dragon, tooth of wolf,
Witch's mummy, maw, and gulf
Of the ravin'd salt-sea shark:
Root of hemlock, digg'd i' th' dark:
Liver of blaspheming Jew,
Gall of goat, and slips of yew,
Sliver'd in the moon's eclipse:
Nose of Turk, and Tartar's lips:
Finger of birth-strangled babe,
Ditch-deliver'd by a drab,
Make the gruel thick, and slab.
Add thereto a tiger's chaudron,
For th' ingredients of our cauldron.
ALL: Double, double, toil and trouble,
Fire burn, and cauldron bubble.
SECOND WITCH : Cool it with a baboon's blood,
Then the charm is firm and good.

Enter Hecat, to the other three Witches.

HECAT: O well done: I commend your pains,
And every one shall share i' th' gains:
And now about the cauldron sing
Like elves and fairies in a ring,
Enchanting all that you put in.

Music and a song: 'Black spirits,' etc.

SECOND WITCH: By the pricking of my thumbs,
Something wicked this way comes:
Open locks, whoever knocks.

Enter Macbeth.

MACBETH: How now you secret, black, and midnight hags?
What is't you do?
ALL : A deed without a name.
MACBETH: I conjure you, by that which you profess,

(Howe'er you come to know it) answer me:
Though you untie the winds, and let them fight
Against the churches: though the yesty waves
Confound and swallow navigation up:
Though bladed corn be lodg'd, and trees blown down,
Though castles topple on their warders' heads:
Though palaces, and pyramids do slope
Their heads to their foundations: though the treasure
Of Nature's germen, tumble all together,
Even till destruction sicken: answer me
To what I ask you.

FIRST WITCH: Speak.

SECOND WITCH: Demand.

THIRD WITCH: We'll answer.

FIRST WITCH: Say, if thou'dst rather hear it from our mouths,
Or from our masters.

MACBETH: Call 'em: let me see 'em.

FIRST WITCH: Pour in sow's blood, that hath eaten
Her nine farrow: grease that's sweaten
From the murderer's gibbet, throw
Into the flame.

ALL : Come high or low:
Thyself and office deftly show.

Thunder. First Apparition, an Armed Head.

MACBETH: Tell me, thou unknown power.

FIRST WITCH: He knows thy thought:
Hear his speech, but say thou nought.

FIRST APPARITION: Macbeth, Macbeth, Macbeth:
Beware Macduff,
Beware the Thane of Fife: dismiss me. Enough.

He descends.

MACBETH: Whate'er thou art, for thy good caution, thanks,
Thou hast harp'd my fear aright. But one word more.

FIRST WITCH: He will not be commanded: here's another,
More potent than the first.

Thunder. Second Apparition, a Bloody Child.

SECOND APPARITION: Macbeth, Macbeth, Macbeth.
MACBETH: Had I three ears, I'ld hear thee.
SECOND APPARITION: Be bloody, bold, and resolute:
Laugh to scorn
The power of man: for none of woman born
Shall harm Macbeth.

Descends.

MACBETH : Then live Macduff: what need I fear of thee?
But yet I'll make assurance double sure,
And take a bond of Fate: thou shalt not live,
That I may tell pale-hearted Fear, it lies;
And sleep in spite of thunder.

Thunder. Third Apparition: a Child crowned, with a tree in his hand.

What is this, that rises like the issue of a King,
And wears upon his baby-brow, the round
And top of sovereignty?
ALL: Listen, but speak not to't.
THIRD APPARITION: Be lion-mettled, proud, and take no care:
Who chafes, who frets, or where conspirers are:
Macbeth shall never vanquish'd be, until
Great Birnam Wood, to high Dunsinane Hill
Shall come against him.

Descends.

MACBETH: That will never be:
Who can impress the forest, bid the tree
Unfix his earth-bound root? Sweet bodements, good:
Rebellion's head, rise never till the Wood
Of Birnam rise, and our high-plac'd Macbeth
Shall live the lease of Nature, pay his breath
To time, and mortal custom. Yet my heart
Throbs to know one thing: tell me, if your Art

Can tell so much: shall Banquo's issue ever
Reign in this Kingdom?
ALL: Seek to know no more.
MACBETH: I will be satisfied. Deny me this,
And an eternal curse fall on you: let me know.
Why sinks that cauldron? and what noise is this?
Oboes.
FIRST WITCH: Show.
SECOND WITCH: Show.
THIRD WITCH: Show.
ALL: Show his eyes, and grieve his heart,
Come like shadows, so depart.
A show of eight Kings, and Banquo last, with a glass in his hand.
MACBETH: Thou art too like the spirit of Banquo: down:
Thy crown does sear mine eye-balls. And thy hair,
Thou other gold-bound brow, is like the first:
A third is like the former. Filthy hags,
Why do you show me this? — A fourth? Start eyes!
What will the line stretch out to th' crack of Doom?
Another yet? A seventh? I'll see no more:
And yet the eighth appears, who bears a glass,
Which shows me many more; and some I see,
That two-fold balls, and treble sceptres carry.
Horrible sight: now I see 'tis true,
For the blood-bolter'd Banquo smiles upon me,
And points at them for his. What? is this so?
FIRST WITCH: Ay Sir, all this is so. But why
Stands Macbeth thus amazedly?
Come sisters, cheer we up his sprites,
And show the best of our delights.
I'll charm the air to give a sound,
While you perform your antic round:
That this great King may kindly say,
Our duties did his welcome pay.

Music. The Witches dance, and vanish.

MACBETH: Where are they? Gone?
Let this pernicious hour,
Stand aye accursed in the Calendar.
Come in, without there.

Enter Lennox.

LENNOX : What's your Grace's will?
MACBETH: Saw you the Weird Sisters?
LENNOX : No my Lord.
MACBETH: Came they not by you?
LENNOX: No indeed my Lord.
MACBETH: Infected be the air whereon they ride,
And damn'd all those that trust them. I did hear
The galloping of horse. Who was't came by?
LENNOX: 'Tis two or three my Lord, that bring you word:
Macduff is fled to England.
MACBETH: Fled to England?
LENNOX: Ay, my good Lord.
MACBETH: Time, thou anticipat'st my dread exploits:
The flighty purpose never is o'ertook
Unless the deed go with it. From this moment,
The very firstlings of my heart shall be
The firstlings of my hand. And even now
To crown my thoughts with acts, be it thought and done:
The Castle of Macduff, I will surprise,
Seize upon Fife: give to th' edge o' th' sword
His wife, his babes, and all unfortunate souls
That trace him in his line. No boasting like a fool,
This deed I'll do, before this purpose cool,
But no more sights. Where are these gentlemen?
Come bring me where they are.

Exeunt.

IV. 2

Enter Macduff's wife, her Son, and Ross.

LADY MACDUFF: What had he done, to make him fly the land?

ROSS: You must have patience Madam.

LADY MACDUFF: He had none:
His flight was madness: when our actions do not,
Our fears do make us traitors.

ROSS: You know not
Whether it was his wisdom, or his fear.

LADY MACDUFF: Wisdom? to leave his wife, to leave his babes,
His mansion, and his titles, in a place
From whence himself does fly? He loves us not,
He wants the natural touch. For the poor wren,
(The most diminutive of birds) will fight,
Her young ones in her nest, against the owl:
All is the fear, and nothing is the love;
As little is the wisdom, where the flight
So runs against all reason.

ROSS: My dearest coz,
I pray you school yourself. But for your husband,
He is noble, wise, judicious, and best knows
The fits o' th' season. I dare not speak much further,
But cruel are the times, when we are traitors
And do not know ourselves: when we hold rumour
From what we fear, yet know not what we fear,
But float upon a wild and violent sea
Each way, and move. I take my leave of you:
Shall not be long but I'll be here again:
Things at the worst will cease, or else climb upward,
To what they were before. My pretty cousin,
Blessing upon you.

LADY MACDUFF: Father'd he is,
And yet he's fatherless.
ROSS: I am so much a fool, should I stay longer
It would be my disgrace, and your discomfort.
I take my leave at once.

Exit Ross.

LADY MACDUFF: Sirrah, your father's dead,
And what will you do now ? How will you live?
SON: As birds do, Mother.
LADY MACDUFF: What with worms, and flies?
SON: With what I get I mean, and so do they.
LADY MACDUFF: Poor bird,
Thou'ldst never fear the net, nor lime,
The pitfall, nor the gin.
SON: Why should I, mother?
Poor birds they are not set for :
My father is not dead for all your saying.
LADY MACDUFF: Yes, he is dead:
How wilt thou do for a father?
SON: Nay how will you do for a husband?
LADY MACDUFF: Why I can buy me twenty at any market.
SON: Then you'll buy 'em to sell again.
LADY MACDUFF: Thou speak'st with all thy wit.
And yet i' faith with wit enough for thee.
SON : Was my father a traitor, Mother?
LADY MACDUFF: Ay, that he was.
SON : What is a traitor?
LADY MACDUFF: Why one that swears, and lies.
SON: And be all traitors, that do so?
LADY MACDUFF: Every one that does so, is a traitor, and must be hang'd.
SON: And must they all be hang'd, that swear and lie?
LADY MACDUFF: Every one.
SON: Who must hang them?
LADY MACDUFF: Why, the honest men.

SON: Then the liars and swearers are fools: for there are liars and swearers enow, to beat the honest men, and hang up them.

LADY MACDUFF : Now God help thee, poor monkey:
But how wilt thou do for a father?

SON : If he were dead, you'ld weep for him: if you would not, it were a good sign, that I should quickly have a new father.

LADY MACDUFF: Poor prattler, how thou talk'st!

Enter a Messenger.

MESSENGER: Bless you fair Dame: I am not to you known.
Though in your state of honour I am perfect;
I doubt some danger does approach you nearly.
If you will take a homely man's advice,
Be not found here: hence with your little ones.
To fright you thus, methinks I am too savage:
To do worse to you, were fell cruelty,
Which is too nigh your person. Heaven preserve you,
I dare abide no longer.

Exit Messenger.

LADY MACDUFF: Whither should I fly?
I have done no harm. But I remember now
I am in this earthly world: where to do harm
Is often laudable, to do good sometime
Accounted dangerous folly. Why then, alas.
Do I put up that womanly defence,
To say I have done no harm ?
What are these faces ?

Enter Murtherers.

FIRST MURDERER: Where is your husband?

LADY MACDUFF: I hope in no place so unsanctified,
Where such as thou mayst find him.

FIRST MURDERER: He's a traitor.

SON: Thou liest thou shag-ear'd villain.

FIRST MURDERER: What you egg?

Young fry of treachery!
SON: He has kill'd me Mother,
Run away I pray you!

Exit crying Murther.

IV. 3

Enter Malcolm and Macduff.

MALCOLM : Let us seek out some desolate shade, and there
Weep our sad bosoms empty.
MACDUFF: Let us rather
Hold fast the mortal sword: and like good men,
Bestride our down-fall'n birthdom: each new morn,
New widows howl, hew orphans cry, new sorrows
Strike heaven on the face, that it resounds
As if it felt with Scotland, and yell'd out
Like syllable of dolour.
MALCOLM: What I believe, I'll wail;
What know, believe; and what I can redress,
As I shall find the time to friend: I will.
What you have spoke, it may be so perchance.
This Tyrant, whose sole name blisters our tongues,
Was once thought honest: you have lov'd him well,
He hath not touch'd you yet. I am young, but something
You may discern of him through me, and wisdom
To offer up a weak, poor innocent lamb
T' appease an angry god.
MACDUFF: I am not treacherous.
MALCOLM: But Macbeth is.
A good and virtuous nature may recoil
In an imperial charge. But I shall crave your pardon:
That which you are, my thoughts cannot transpose;
Angels are bright still, though the brightest fell.
Though all things foul, would wear the brows of grace
Yet Grace must still look so.

MACDUFF: I have lost my hopes.
MALCOLM: Perchance even there
  Where I did find my doubts.
  Why in that rawness left you wife, and child?
  Those precious motives, those strong knots of love,
  Without leave-taking? I pray you,
  Let not my jealousies, be your dishonours,
  But mine own safeties: you may be rightly just,
  Whatever I shall think.
MACDUFF: Bleed, bleed poor Country.
  Great Tyranny, lay thou thy basis sure,
  For goodness dare not check thee: wear thou thy wrongs,
  The title is affeer'd. Fare thee well Lord,
  I would not be the villain that thou think'st,
  For the whole space that's in the Tyrant's grasp,
  And the rich East to boot.
MALCOLM: Be not offended:
  I speak not as in absolute fear of you:
  I think our country sinks beneath the yoke,
  It weeps, it bleeds, and each new day a gash
  Is added to her wounds. I think withal,
  There would be hands uplifted in my right:
  And here from gracious England have I offer
  Of goodly thousands. But for all this,
  When I shall tread upon the Tyrant's head,
  Or wear it on my sword; yet my poor Country
  Shall have more vices than it had before,
  More suffer, and more sundry ways than ever,
  By him that shall succeed.
MACDUFF: What should he be?
MALCOLM: It is myself I mean: in whom I know
  All the particulars of vice so grafted,
  That when they shall be open'd, black Macbeth
  Will seem as pure as snow, and the poor State
  Esteem him as a lamb, being compar'd
  With my confineless harms.

MACDUFF: Not in the legions
Of horrid Hell, can come a devil more damn'd
In evils, to top Macbeth.
MALCOLM : I grant him bloody,
Luxurious, avaricious, false, deceitful,
Sudden, malicious, smacking of every sin
That has a name. But there's no bottom, none
In my voluptuousness: your wives, your daughters.
Your matrons, and your maids, could not fill up
The cistern of my lust, and my desire
All continent impediments would o'erbear
That did oppose my will. Better Macbeth,
Than such an one to reign.
MACDUFF: Boundless intemperance
In Nature is a tyranny: it hath been
Th' untimely emptying of the happy throne,
And fall of many Kings. But fear not yet
To take upon you what is yours: you may
Convey your pleasures in a spacious plenty,
And yet seem cold. The time you may so hoodwink:
We have willing dames enough: there cannot be
That vulture in you, to devour so many
As will to greatness dedicate themselves,
Finding it so inclin'd.
MALCOLM: With this, there grows
In my most ill-compos'd affection, such
A stanchless avarice, that were I King,
I should cut off the Nobles for their lands,
Desire his jewels, and this other's house,
And my more-having, would be as a sauce
To make me hunger more, that I should forge
Quarrels unjust against the good and loyal,
Destroying them for wealth.
MACDUFF: This avarice
Sticks deeper: grows with more pernicious root

Than summer-seeming lust: and it hath been
The sword of our slain Kings: yet do not fear,
Scotland hath foisons, to fill up your will
Of your mere own. All these are portable,
With other graces weigh'd.

MALCOLM: But I have none. The king-becoming graces,
As justice, verity, temperance, stableness,
Bounty, perseverance, mercy, lowliness,
Devotion, patience, courage, fortitude,
I have no relish of them, but abound
In the division of each several crime,
Acting it many ways. Nay, had I power, I should
Pour the sweet milk of concord, into Hell,
Uproar the universal peace, confound
All unity on earth.

MACDUFF: O Scotland, Scotland.

MALCOLM : If such a one be fit to govern, speak:
I am as I have spoken.

MACDUFF: Fit to govern? No not to live. O Nation miserable!
With an untitled Tyrant, bloody scepter'd,
When shalt thou see thy wholesome days again?
Since that the truest issue of thy Throne
By his own interdiction stands accus'd,
And does blaspheme his breed? Thy Royal Father
Was a most sainted King: the Queen that bore thee,
Oftener upon her knees, than on her feet,
Died every day she liv'd. Fare thee well,
These evils thou repeat'st upon thyself,
Have banish'd me from Scotland. O my breast,
Thy hope ends here.

MALCOLM: Macduff, this noble passion,
Child of integrity, hath from my soul
Wip'd the black scruples, reconcil'd my thoughts
To thy good truth, and honour. Devilish Macbeth,
By many of these trains, hath sought to win me

Into his power: and modest wisdom plucks me
From over-credulous haste: but God above
Deal between thee and me; for even now
I put myself to thy direction, and
Unspeak mine own detraction. Here abjure
The taints, and blames I laid upon myself,
For strangers to my nature. I am yet
Unknown to woman, never was forsworn,
Scarcely have coveted what was mine own,
At no time broke my faith, would not betray
The Devil to his fellow, and delight
No less in truth than life. My first false speaking
Was this upon myself. What I am truly
Is thine, and my poor Country's to command:
Whither indeed, before thy here approach
Old Siward with ten thousand warlike men
Already at a point, was setting forth:
Now we'll together, and the chance of goodness
Be like our warranted quarrel. Why are you silent?

MACDUFF: Such welcome, and unwelcome things at once
'Tis hard, to reconcile.

Enter a Doctor.

MALCOLM: Well, more anon. Comes the King forth
I pray you?

DOCTOR: Ay Sir: there are a crew of wretched souls
That stay his cure: their malady convinces
The great assay of Art. But at his touch,
Such sanctity hath Heaven given his hand,
They presently amend.

MALCOLM: I thank you doctor.

Exit.

MACDUFF: What's the disease he means?

MALCOLM: 'Tis call'd the Evil.
A most miraculous work in this good King,
Which often since my here remain in England,

I have seen him do: how he solicits Heaven
Himself best knows: but strangely-visited people,
All swoln and ulcerous, pitiful to the eye,
The mere despair of surgery, he cures,
Hanging a golden stamp about their necks,
Put on with holy prayers, and 'tis spoken,
To the succeeding royalty he leaves
The healing benediction. With this strange virtue,
He hath a heavenly gift of prophecy,
And sundry blessings hang about his Throne,
That speak him full of grace.

Enter Ross.

MACDUFF: See who comes here.
MALCOLM: My countryman : but yet I know him not.
MACDUFF: My ever gentle cousin, welcome hither.
MALCOLM : I know him now. Good God betimes remove
The means that makes us strangers.
ROSS: Sir, amen.
MACDUFF: Stands Scotland where it did?
ROSS: Alas poor country,
Almost afraid to know itself. It cannot
Be call'd our mother, but our grave; where nothing
But who knows nothing, is once seen to smile:
Where sighs, and groans, and shrieks that rent the air
Are made, not mark'd: where violent sorrow seems
A modern ecstasy: the dead man's knell,
Is there scarce ask'd for who, and good men's lives
Expire before the flowers in their caps,
Dying, or ere they sicken.
MACDUFF: O relation too nice, and yet too true.
MALCOLM: What's the newest grief?
ROSS: That of an hour's age, doth hiss the speaker,
Each minute teems a new one.
MACDUFF: How does my wife?
ROSS: Why well.

MACDUFF: And all my children?
ROSS: Well too.
MACDUFF: The Tyrant has not batter'd at their peace?
ROSS: No, they were well at peace, when I did leave 'em.
MACDUFF : Be not a niggard of your speech: how goes't?
ROSS: When I came hither to transport the tidings
Which I have heavily borne, there ran a rumour
Of many worthy fellows, that were out,
Which was to my belief witness'd the rather,
For that I saw the Tyrant's power a-foot.
Now is the time of help: your eye in Scotland
Would create soldiers, make our women fight,
To doff their dire distresses.
MALCOLM: Be't their comfort
We are coming thither: gracious England hath
Lent us good Siward, and ten thousand men,
An older, and a better soldier, none
That Christendom gives out.
ROSS: Would I could answer
This comfort with the like. But I have words
That would be howl'd out in the desert air,
Where hearing should not latch them.
MACDUFF: What concern they,
The general cause, or is it a fee-grief
Due to some single breast?
ROSS: No mind that's honest
But in it shares some woe, though the main part
Pertains to you alone.
MACDUFF: If it be mine
Keep it not from me, quickly let me have it.
ROSS: Let not your ears despise my tongue for ever.
Which shall possess them with the heaviest sound
That ever yet they heard.
MACDUFF: Humh: 1 guess at it.
ROSS: Your Castle is surpris'd: your wife, and babes

Savagely slaughter'd: to relate the manner
Were on the quarry of these murther'd deer
To add the death of you.

MALCOLM: Merciful Heavens:
What man, ne'er pull your hat upon your brows :
Give sorrow words; the grief that does not speak,
Whispers the o'er-fraught heart, and bids it break.

MACDUFF: My children too?

ROSS: Wife, children, servants, all that could be found.

MACDUFF: And I must be from thence? My wife kill'd too?

ROSS: I have said.

MALCOLM: Be comforted.
Let's make us medicines of our great revenge,
To cure this deadly grief.

MACDUFF: He has no children. All my pretty ones?
Did you say All? O hell-kite! All?
What, All my pretty chickens, and their dam
At one fell swoop?

MALCOLM: Dispute it like a man.

MACDUFF: I shall do so:
But I must also feel it as a man;
I cannot but remember such things were
That were most precious to me: did Heaven look on,
And would not take their part? Sinful Macduff,
They were all struck for thee: naught that I am,
Not for their own demerits, but for mine
Fell slaughter on their souls: Heaven rest them now.

MALCOLM: Be this the whetstone of your sword, let grief
Convert to anger: blunt not the heart, enrage it.

MACDUFF: O I could play the woman with mine eyes,
And braggart with my tongue. But gentle Heavens,
Cut short all intermission: front to front,
Bring thou this fiend of Scotland, and myself;
Within my sword's length set him, if he scape
Heaven forgive him too.

MALCOLM: This tune goes manly:
Come go we to the King, our power is ready,
Our lack is nothing but our leave. Macbeth
Is ripe for shaking, and the Powers above
Put on their instruments: receive what cheer you may,
The night is long, that never finds the day.

Exeunt.

V. 1

Enter a Doctor of Physic, and a Waiting Gentlewoman.

DOCTOR: I have two nights watch'd with you, but can perceive no truth in your report. When was it she last walk'd?

GENTLEWOMAN: Since his Majesty went into the field, I have seen her rise from her bed, throw her nightgown upon her, unlock her closet, take forth paper, fold it, write upon't, read it, afterwards seal it, and again return to bed; yet all this while in a most fast sleep.

DOCTOR : A great perturbation in nature, to receive at once the benefit of sleep, and do the effects of watching. In this slumbery agitation, besides her walking, and other actual performances, what (at any time) have you heard her say?

GENTLEWOMAN: That sir, which I will not report after her.

DOCTOR: You may to me, and 'tis most meet you should.

GENTLEWOMAN: Neither to you, nor any one, having no witness to confirm my speech.

Enter Lady Macbeth, with a taper.

Lo you, here she comes: this is her very guise, and upon my life fast asleep: observe her, stand close.

DOCTOR: How came she by that light?

GENTLEWOMAN: Why it stood by her: she has light by her continually, 'tis her command.

DOCTOR: You see her eyes are open.

GENTLEWOMAN: Ay but their sense are shut.

DOCTOR: What is it she does now?

Look how she rubs her hands.

GENTLEWOMAN: It is an accustom'd action with her, to seem thus washing her hands: I have known her continue in this a quarter of an hour.

LADY MACBETH: Yet here's a spot.

DOCTOR: Hark, she speaks, I will set down what comes from her, to satisfy my remembrance the more strongly.

LADY MACBETH: Out damned spot: out I say. One: two: why then 'tis time to do 't: Hell is murky. Fie, my Lord, fie, a soldier, and afear'd? what need we fear? who knows it, when none can call our power to accompt: yet who would have thought the old man to have had so much blood in him.

DOCTOR: Do you mark that?

LADY MACBETH: The Thane of Fife, had a wife: where is she now? What will these hands ne'er be clean? No more o' that my Lord, no more o' that: you mar all with this starting.

DOCTOR: Go to, go to:
You have known what you should not.

GENTLEWOMAN : She has spoke what she should not, I am sure of that: Heaven knows what she has known.

LADY MACBETH: Here's the smell of the blood still: all the perfumes of Arabia will not sweeten this little hand. Oh, oh, oh.

DOCTOR : What a sigh is there! The heart is sorely charg'd.

GENTLEWOMAN: I would not have such a heart in my bosom, for the dignity of the whole body.

DOCTOR: Well, well, well.

GENTLEWOMAN: Pray God it be sir.

DOCTOR: This disease is beyond my practice: yet I have known those which have walk'd in their sleep, who have died holily in their beds.

LADY MACBETH: Wash your hands, put on your nightgown, look not so pale: I tell you yet again Banquo's buried; he cannot come out on's grave.

DOCTOR: Even so?

LADY MACBETH: To bed, to bed: there's knocking at the gate: come, come, come, come, give me your hand: what's done, cannot be undone. To bed, to bed, to bed.

Exit Lady Macbeth.

DOCTOR: Will she go now to bed?

GENTLEWOMAN: Directly.

DOCTOR : Foul whisperings are abroad: unnatural deeds
Do breed unnatural troubles: infected minds
To their deaf pillows will discharge their secrets:
More needs she the divine, than the physician:
God, God forgive us all. Look after her,
Remove from her the means of all annoyance,
And still keep eyes upon her: so good night,
My mind she has mated, and amaz'd my sight.
I think, but dare not speak.

GENTLEWOMAN: Good night good doctor.

Exeunt.

V. 2

Drum and colours. Enter Menteith, Caithness, Angus, Lennox, Soldiers.

MENTIETH : The English power is near, led on by Malcolm,
His uncle Siward, and the good Macduff.
Revenges burn in them: for their dear causes
Would to the bleeding, and the grim alarm
Excite the mortified man.

ANGUS: Near Birnam wood
Shall we well meet them, that way are they coming.

CAITHNESS : Who knows if Donalbain be with his brother?

LENNOX : For certain sir, he is not: I have a file
Of all the gentry; there is Siward's son,
And many unrough youths, that even now
Protest their first of manhood.

MENTIETH:What does the tyrant?

CAITHNESS: Great Dunsinane he strongly fortifies:

Some say he's mad: others, that lesser hate him,
Do call it valiant fury, but for certain
He cannot buckle his distemper'd cause
Within the belt of rule.
ANGUS: Now does he feel
His secret murthers sticking on his hands,
Now minutely revolts upbraid his faith-breach:
Those he commands, move only in command,
Nothing in love: now does he feel his title
Hang loose about him, like a giant's robe
Upon a dwarfish thief.
MENTIETH: Who then shall blame
His pester'd senses to recoil, and start,
When all that is within him, does condemn
Itself, for being there?
CAITHNESS: Well, march we on,
To give obedience, where 'tis truly ow'd:
Meet we the medicine of the sickly weal,
And with him pour we in our country's purge,
Each drop of us.
LENNOX: Or so much as it needs,
To dew the sovereign flower, and drown the weeds:
Make we our march towards Birnam.
Exeunt marching.

V. 3

Enter Macbeth, Doctor, and Attendants.
MACBETH: Bring me no more reports, let them fly all:
Till Birnam wood remove to Dunsinane,
I cannot taint with fear. What's the boy Malcolm?
Was he not born of woman? The spirits that know
All mortal consequences, have pronounc'd me thus:
Fear not Macbeth, no man that's born of woman
Shall e'er have power upon thee. Then fly false Thanes,

And mingle with the English epicures;
The mind I sway by, and the heart I bear,
Shall never sag with doubt, nor shake with fear.

Enter Servant.

The Devil damn thee black, thou cream-fac'd loon:
Where got'st thou that goose look?

SERVANT: There is ten thousand.

MACBETH: Geese villain?

SERVANT: Soldiers sir.

MACBETH: Go prick thy face, and over-red thy fear
Thou lily-liver'd boy. What soldiers, patch?
Death of thy soul, those linen cheeks of thine
Are councillors to fear. What soldiers whey-face?

SERVANT: The English force, so please you.

MACBETH: Take thy face hence.

Exit Servant.

Seyton, I am sick at heart,
When I behold: Seyton, I say, this push
Will cheer me ever, or disseat me now.
I have liv'd long enough; my way of life
Is fall'n into the sear, the yellow leaf,
And that which should accompany old age,
As honour, love, obedience, troops of friends,
I must not look to have: but in their stead,
Curses, not loud but deep, mouth-honour, breath
Which the poor heart would fain deny, and dare not.
Seyton !

Enter Seyton.

SEYTON: What's your gracious pleasure?

MACBETH: What news more?

SEYTON: All is confirm'd my Lord, which was reported.

MACBETH: I'll fight, till from my bones, my flesh be hack'd.
Give me my armour.

SEYTON: 'Tis not needed yet.

MACBETH: I'll put it on:

Send out moe horses, skirr the country round,
Hang those that talk of fear. Give me mine armour:
How does your patient, doctor?
DOCTOR: Not so sick my Lord,
As she is troubled with thick-coming fancies
That keep her from her rest.
MACBETH: Cure her of that:
Canst thou not minister to a mind diseas'd.
Pluck from the memory a rooted sorrow,
Raze out the written troubles of the brain,
And with some sweet oblivious antidote
Cleanse the stuff'd bosom, of that perilous stuff.
Which weighs upon the heart?
DOCTOR: Therein the patient
Must minister to himself.
MACBETH: Throw physic to the dogs, I'll none of it.
Come, put mine armour on: give me my staff:
Seyton, send out: doctor, the Thanes fly from me :
Come sir, dispatch. If thou couldst doctor, cast
The water of my land, find her disease,
And purge it to a sound and pristine health,
I would applaud thee to the very echo,
That should applaud again. Pull't off I say,
What rhubarb, senna, or what purgative drug
Would scour these English hence: hear'st thou of them?
DOCTOR: Ay my good Lord: your royal preparation
Makes us hear something.
MACBETH: Bring it after me:
I will not be afraid of death and bane,
Till Birnam Forest come to Dunsinane.
DOCTOR: Were I from Dunsinane away, and clear,
Profit again should hardly draw me here.

Exeunt.

V. 4

Drum and colours. Enter Malcolm, Siward, Macduff, Siward's son, Mentieth, Caithness, Angus, and Soldiers marching.

MALCOLM: Cousins, I hope the days are near at hand
That chambers will be safe.
MENTIETH: We doubt it nothing.
SIWARD: What wood is this before us?
MENTIETH: The wood of Birnam.
MALCOLM : Let every soldier hew him down a bough,
And bear't before him, thereby shall we shadow
The numbers of our host, and make discovery
Err in report of us.
SOLDIERS: It shall be done.
SIWARD : We learn no other, but the confident Tyrant
Keeps still in Dunsinane, and will endure
Our setting down before't.
MALCOLM: 'Tis his main hope:
For where there is advantage to be given,
Both more and less have given him the revolt,
And none serve with him, but constrained things,
Whose hearts are absent too.
MACDUFF: Let our just censures
Attend the true event, and put we on
Industrious soldiership,
SIWARD: The time approaches,
That will with due decision make us know
What we shall say we have, and what we owe:
Thoughts speculative, their unsure hopes relate,
But certain issue, strokes must arbitrate,
Towards which, advance the war.

Exeunt marching.

V. 5

Enter Macbeth, Seyton, and Soldiers, with drum and colours.

MACBETH: Hang out our banners on the outward walls,
The cry is still, they come: our Castle's strength
Will laugh a siege to scorn: here let them lie,
Till famine and the ague eat them up:
Were they not forc'd with those that should be ours,
We might have met them dareful, beard to beard,
And beat them backward home. What is that noise?

A cry within of women.

SEYTON: It is the cry of women, my good Lord.

MACBETH: I have almost forgot the taste of fears:
The time has been, my senses would have cool'd
To hear a night-shriek, and my fell of hair
Would at a dismal treatise rouse, and stir
As life were in't. I have supp'd full with horrors,
Direness familiar to my slaughterous thoughts
Cannot once start me. Wherefore was that cry?

SEYTON: The Queen, my Lord, is dead.

MACBETH: She should have died hereafter;
There would have been a time for such a word:
To-morrow, and to-morrow, and to-morrow,
Creeps in this petty pace from day to day,
To the last syllable of recorded time:
And all our yesterdays, have lighted fools
The way to dusty death. Out, out, brief candle,
Life's but a walking shadow, a poor player,
That struts and frets his hour upon the stage,
And then is heard no more. It is a tale
Told by an idiot, full of sound and fury
Signifying nothing.

Enter a Messenger.

Thou comest to use thy tongue: thy story quickly.

MESSENGER: Gracious my Lord,

I should report that which I say I saw,
But know not how to do it.
MACBETH: Well, say sir.
MESSENGER: As I did stand my watch upon the hill,
I look'd toward Birnam, and anon methought
The Wood began to move.
MACBETH: Liar, and slave.
MESSENGER: Let me endure your wrath, if't be not so:
Within this three mile may you see it coming.
I say, a moving grove.
MACBETH: If thou speak'st false,
Upon the next tree shalt thou hang alive
Till famine cling thee: if thy speech be sooth,
I care not if thou dost for me as much.
I pull in resolution, and begin
To doubt th' equivocation of the fiend,
That lies like truth. Fear not, till Birnam Wood
Do come to Dunsinane; and now a wood
Comes toward Dunsinane. Arm, arm, and out,
If this which he avouches, does appear,
There is nor flying hence, nor tarrying here.
I 'gin to be aweary of the sun,
And wish th' estate o' th' world were now undone.
Ring the alarum-bell, blow wind, come wrack,
At least we'll die with harness on our back.
Exeunt.

V. 6

Drums and colours.
Enter Malcolm, Siward, Macduff, and their Army, with boughs.
MALCOLM: Now near enough:
Your leavy screens throw down,
And show like those you are: you, worthy uncle,

Shall with my cousin your right noble son
Lead our first battle. Worthy Macduff, and we
Shall take upon's what else remains to do,
According to our order.

SIWARD: Fare you well:
Do we but find the tyrant's power to-night,
Let us be beaten, if we cannot fight.

MACDUFF: Make all our trumpets speak, give them all breath,
Those clamorous harbingers of blood, and death.

Exeunt.

Alarums continued.

V. 7

Enter Macbeth.

MACBETH: They have tied me to a stake, I cannot fly,
But bear-like I must fight the course. What's he
That was not born of woman? Such a one
Am I to fear, or none.

Enter young Siward.

YOUNG SIWARD: What is thy name?

MACBETH: Thou'lt be afraid to hear it.

YOUNG SIWARD: No: though thou call'st thyself a hotter name
Than any is in hell.

MACBETH: My name's Macbeth.

YOUNG SIWARD: The devil himself could not pronounce a title
More hateful to mine ear.

MACBETH: No: nor more fearful.

YOUNG SIWARD: Thou best abhorred Tyrant, with my sword
I'll prove the lie thou speak'st.

Fight, and young Siward slain.

MACBETH: Thou wast born of woman:
But swords I smile at, weapons laugh to scorn,

Brandish'd by man that's of a woman born.

Exit.

Alarums. Enter Macduff.

MACDUFF: That way the noise is: Tyrant show thy face;
If thou be'st slain, and with no stroke of mine,
My wife and children's ghosts will haunt me still:
I cannot strike at wretched kerns, whose arms
Are hir'd to bear their staves; either thou Macbeth,
Or else my sword with an unbatter'd edge
I sheathe again undeeded. There thou shouldst be,
By this great clatter, one of greatest note
Seems bruited. Let me find him Fortune,
And more I beg not.

Exit. Alarums.

Enter Malcolm and Siward.

SIWARD: This way my Lord, the Castle' gently render'd:
The Tyrant's people, on both sides do fight,
The noble Thanes do bravely in the war,
The day almost itself professes yours,
And little is to do.

MALCOLM: We have met with foes
That strike beside us.

SIWARD: Enter Sir, the Castle.

Exeunt. Alarum.

Enter Macbeth.

MACBETH: Why should I play the Roman fool, and die
On mine own sword? whiles I see lives, the gashes
Do better upon them.

Enter Macduff.

MACDUFF: Turn hell-hound, turn.

MACBETH: Of all men else I have avoided thee:
But get thee back, my soul is too much charg'd
With blood of thine already.

MACDUFF: I have no words,

My voice is in my sword, thou bloodier villain
Than terms can give thee out.

Fight. Alarum.

MACBETH: Thou losest labour;
As easy mayst thou the intrenchant air
With thy keen sword impress, as make me bleed:
Let fall thy blade on vulnerable crests,
I bear a charmed life, which must not yield
To one of woman born.

MACDUFF: Despair thy charm,
And let the Angel whom thou still hast serv'd
Tell thee, Macduff was from his mother's womb
Untimely ripp'd.

MACBETH: Accursed be that tongue that tells me so;
For it hath cow'd my better part of man:
And be these juggling fiends no more believ'd.
That palter with us in a double sense,
That keep the word of promise to our ear,
And break it to our hope. I'll not fight with thee.

MACDUFF: Then yield thee coward,
And live to be the show, and gaze o' th' time.
We'll have thee, as our rarer monsters are,
Painted upon a pole, and underwrit,
Here may you see the tyrant.

MACBETH: I will not yield
To kiss the ground before young Malcolm's feet,
And to be baited with the rabble's curse.
Though Birnam Wood be come to Dunsinane,
And thou oppos'd, being of no woman born,
Yet I will try the last. Before my body,
I throw my warlike shield: lay on Macduff,
And damn'd be him, that first cries hold, enough.

Exeunt fighting. Alarums.

Retreat and flourish. Enter with drum and colours, Malcolm, Siward, Ross, Thanes, and Soldiers.

MALCOLM: I would the friends we miss, were safe arriv'd.
SIWARD: Some must go off: and yet by these I see,
So great a day as this is cheaply bought.
MALCOLM : Macduff is missing, and your noble son.
ROSS : Your son my Lord, has paid a soldier's debt;
He only liv'd but till he was a man.
The which no sooner had his prowess confirm'd
In the unshrinking station where he fought,
But like a man he died.
SIWARD: Then he is dead?
ROSS : Ay, and brought off the field: your cause of sorrow
Must not be measur'd by his worth, for then
It hath no end.
SIWARD: Had he his hurts before?
ROSS: Ay, on the front.
SIWARD: Why then, God's soldier be he:
Had as I as many sons, as I have hairs,
I would not wish them to a fairer death:
And so his knell is knoll'd.
MALCOLM: He's worth more sorrow,
And that I'll spend for him.
SIWARD: He's worth no more,
They say he parted well, and paid his score,
And so God be with him. Here comes newer comfort.

Enter Macduff with Macbeth's head.

MACDUFF: Hail King, for so thou art.
Behold where stands
The usurper's cursed head: the time is free:
I see thee compass'd with thy Kingdom's pearl,
That speak my salutation in their minds:
Whose voices I desire aloud with mine.
Hail King of Scotland.
ALL: Hail King of Scotland.

Flourish.

MALCOLM : We shall not spend a large expense of time,
Before we reckon with your several loves,
And make us even with you. My Thanes and kinsmen
Henceforth be Earls, the first that ever Scotland
In such an honour nam'd. What's more to do,
Which would be planted newly with the time,
As calling home our exil'd friends abroad,
That fled the snares of watchful tyranny,
Producing forth the cruel ministers
Of this dead butcher, and his fiend-like Queen,
Who (as 'tis thought) by self and violent hands,
Took off her life. This, and what needful else
That calls upon us, by the grace of Grace,
We will perform in measure, time, and place:
So thanks to all at once, and to each one,
Whom we invite, to see us crown'd at Scone.

Flourish. Exeunt omnes.

GLOSSARY

addition: a title of honour added to the name, so 'honour'
address'd: made ready
admir'd: wondered at
affeer'd: confirmed
all-thing: in every way
anon: 'I am coming'
annoyance: harm
antic: fantastic
approve: demonstrate
assay: effort
avouch: proclaim

badg'd: lit. wearing a badge of blood
bane: destruction
bare-fac'd: without concealment
battle: division (of an army)
beguile: deceive
beldams: ugly old women
benison: blessing
blood-bolter'd: matted with blood
bodements: prophecies
borne: managed
botches: flaws
break: reveal
breech'd: covered as with breeches
brinded: branded, striped
bruited: noised abroad

cabin'd: confined in a small room
card: the card marking the points of the compass
casing: enclosing
cast: throw up
charg'd: burdened
chaudron: entrails
choppy: chapped
chough: jackdaw
clear: innocent
clearness: freedom from suspicion
clept: called
cling: wither
closet: chest, used for private papers
coign of vantage: convenient corner
composition: agreement, terms of peace
compt: account, which must be produced at the audit

consent: party
continent: containing, restraining
convince: overpower
corporal: bodily
cours'd: pursued
coz: cousin, kinsman
cracks: cannon-balls
crests: heads
cribb'd: confined in a crib
cross'd: thwarted

dear: heartfelt
demi-wolves: half-dog, half-wolf
dispute: strive against
distance: hate
doubt: suspect
Doom: doomsday
dudgeon: handle

earnest: a token payment on account of the main sum due
ecstasy: madness, any strong emotion
expedition: haste

faculties: powers
fantastical: existing only in the fantasy, a creation of the imagination
farrow: litter
favour: face
fell: skin
file: list
fil'd: defiled
flaw: gust of wind
flighty: fleet
forbid: accursed
foisons: abundance
franchis'd: free
furbish'd: newly made ready

gall: bitterness
get: beget
grac'd: full of grace
gulf: stomach

harness: armour
Harpier: a familiar spirit
Hecat: so spelt (and pronounced) in the Folio, one of the goddesses in the underworld
hie: 'hasten
house-keeper: watch-dog
hurly-burly: confusion
husbandry: confusion
Hyrcan: Caspian

incarnadine: make red
initiate: belonging to a novice
interdiction: exclusion
intermission: interval
intrenchant: that cannot be cut
invention: falsehood

jump: risk
jutty frieze: projection on a

building
largess: gift of money
latch: catch
lated: belated
lighted: newly come to earth
lily-liver'd: cowardly
limited: allotted
line: aid
lodg'd: (of corn) laid flat
luxurious: vicious

magot-pies: magpies
mansionry: home
mated: confounded
maw: jaw
measure: quantity of drink, so 'toast'
metaphysical: supernatural
mettle: the same word as 'metal', hard substance, iron disposition
minion: darling
missives: messengers
moe: more
mortified: dead
nave: navel
nice: fastidious
nightgown: dressing-gown
nonpareil: without a parallel

oblivious: causing for getful-ness
obscure bird: the owl
offices: (l) servants' quarters (2) duties
old: slang for 'any amount of'
overcome: overshadow
owe: own

palpable: perceptible by the senses
patch: fool
pauser: that which restrains
peak: waste away
pent-house: a lean-to shed, so 'pent-house' lid = eyelid
pester'd: troubled
physics pain: cures trouble
posset: hot drink, made of wine or ale and milk
posters: travelling post-haste
power: army
present: immediate
pretence: plot, design
proof: armour
purveyor: fore-runner

quarry: heap of slain after a hunt
quell: murder

rapt: entranced
ravin: prey on
rawness: haste
register'd: recorded
remorse: pity
roof'd: under the roof, present
rooky: murky
round: dance
rugged: rough
scarf up: blindfold

seated: fixed
security: false sense of safety
self-abuse: self-deception
sensible: perceived by the senses
sere: dry
sewer: server
shaft: arrow
shard-borne: carried on its shiny wings
shough: shaggy-haired dog
sightless: invisible
skipping: nimble
skirr: scour
slab: thick, muddy
sleave: skein of silk
sleek: make smooth
sleights: tricks
sliver'd: torn off
speculation: power of sight
stamp: coin or medal, stamped with the King's image
still: always
storehouse: tomb

tending: attendance
Thane: a title corresponding to Earl
thralls: serfs
titles: possessions
top: crown
trains: enticements
trenched: gashed
tugg'd with: pulled about by
unlineal: belonging to another descent
unrough: smooth-chinned
utterance: uttermost

virtue: power
vizards: masks
vouch'd: warranted
wassail: carousing
water-rugs: dogs used to the water
weal: commonwealth
wound up: completed

yesty: frothy